D1564472

SMALL-TOWN BASEBALL
IN THE DIRTY
30s

R O B E R T   A S H E

NIMBUS
PUBLISHING

Nimbus Publishing Limited
P.O. Box 9301, Station A
Halifax, Nova Scotia
B3K 5N5

Cover design: Bruce Kierstead, GDA, Halifax
Interior design: Steven Slipp, GDA, Halifax
Cover photograph: *Halifax Herald*, 1949, Nova Scotia Sport Heritage Centre
Back-cover photograph: N.B. Sports Hall of Fame

Canadian Cataloguing in Publication Data

Ashe, Robert

Even the Babe came to play

Includes index.
ISBN 0-921054-96-3

1. Baseball—New Brunswick—St. Stephen—History. I. Title.
GV863.15.S73A83 1991 796.357'09715'33 C91-097637-6

Printed and bound in Canada

6.00

CONTENTS

To those who played

ACKNOWLEDGMENTS

Countless people helped with this book, each contributing information and insights. Librarians, museum employees, photographers and professors all assisted in my research, usually in the regular course of their work. Still, there are some special acknowledgments I'd like to make.

Dr. Roger Bird, of the School of Journalism at Carleton University in Ottawa, provided endless encouragement as I waded through oceans of clippings and transcriptions. The editor, Susan LeBlanc, and Nancy Robb and Jane Plant, of Nimbus Publishing, worked nights and weekends to meet deadlines. My wife, Brenda, offered her patience and support, especially during the writing stages of the book.

And finally, thanks must go to the players who invited me into their homes and shared with me the prime of their lives. It is really their book.

Robert Ashe
June 1991

INTRODUCTION

I T WAS A TIME when the summer morning cleansed and made everything young, when the sense of self was embedded in the sense of community, when neighbors cared. It was a time when an octogenarian from Halifax chided athletes for "doping themselves to run a faster marathon with all crazy mixtures, sugar, glucose, even yeast cakes," when newspaper advertisements reproved "skinniness," when Tudor cigarettes—25 for 25 cents—assured smokers that "you get out of a cigarette what the maker puts into it."

It was also a time of personal strife across Canada, when families ruptured and spirits wilted, when men in their prime were filed and forgotten in relief camps.

But the Canadian experience during the Great Depression of the 1930s was not uniform. While most of the country ached, the Maritimes, a region accustomed to a standard of living well below the national mean, knew poverty as a constant companion.

The degree to which the Maritimes suffered during the Depression is a matter of historical debate. While some data indicates the Depression was less crippling in the region, many historians disagree, calling such a view carefully crafted mythology.

"The myth was partly created by defenders of the region," writes historian E. R. Forbes. "In the late 1920s politicians, board of trade leaders, and newspapermen [campaigned] to counter the negative image of their economy projected by the earlier Maritimes Rights propaganda and to attract investment in a period of economic expansion. When their tactics appeared to pay dividends ... Maritime leaders met renewed depression by increasing the urgency of their campaign.

"The statistics of the period," Forbes continues, "do not support the myth that the Maritimes suffered less from the depression than did the rest of Canada."

Complicating matters is the fact that even within the region the effect was not homogeneous. While some communities virtually collapsed, others seemed immune to the economic virus.

Probably the most blessed of all Maritime towns during the Great Depression was St. Stephen, an economically diverse centre of about 3,400 nestled in the southwestern corner of New Brunswick, on the Maine border. Calais, Maine, a town of similar size, sat directly across the St. Croix River and gave the area an international air, and St. Stephen a resolute nationalism.

Charming and virile, built straight and purposefully where nature had placed a beautiful long river, a lush valley and bountiful forests, St. Stephen was a town in harmony with its appearance. It was a community with an enduring rural grace unmoved by the difficult times, and from the Depression's onset few complained that fate had placed them in St. Stephen. It was a town that had everything.

St. Stephen had even acquired an amateur baseball team in 1930. Furnished with players from St. Stephen, Calais, and neighboring Milltown, New Brunswick, it would be an extraordinary team well suited to the time and to the community. From 1930 to 1939, when war forced its disbandment, the team played under three names and won nine provincial and seven Maritime amateur championships— a record unmatched in Canada at that level of competition. Yet it has been a feat ignored.

The most formidable barrier to national recognition was that the St. Stephen club never played a Canadian team from outside the Maritimes. Nor did the club ever play a game in Halifax, the region's largest centre. Surviving players deeply regret this absence of outside competition. Many still feel that a national series of games would have yielded them their due recognition.

So how good were these champions from St. Stephen? Good enough to challenge a major league ball team and outscore them over the final seven innings. Good enough to defeat professional touring black American teams. Good enough to have one player knock on the door of a big league career, and enable at least four others to come reasonably close.

Yet, especially by today's standards, Maritime amateur—or senior—baseball was crude. Gloves were flat leather mittens with narrow webbing and padded palms that required players to square their body to the ball, rather than to flick out their gloves automatically as ballplayers do today. In the 1930s, players fielded with two hands. "If you caught a ball with just one hand," recalls one infielder, "the boys used to shout, 'Cut the other hand off!'" Batting helmets were not worn and hitting gloves were unknown. Uniforms were usually hand-me-downs, often holey and grimy, sometimes oddly colored and frequently ill-fitting.

The equipment was nevertheless apt for the eclectic group that used it. Amateur baseball was a domain for young males with old vices, but it also offered initial public exposure for a generation of men soon to lead their communities.

Some ballplayers were national champions in other sports, while others were hopeless klutzes who took refuge in right field. Indeed, the chasm in ability between the best players and the average players was great on all but the very top teams. Rudiments of the sport were often disregarded, and contests were decided by brute force—home runs and fastballs.

The better teams, however, had an additional weapon. In St. Stephen, where it was abundant, they called it "inside baseball," and it included everything from keen anticipation to trickery. Whatever, it set St. Stephen teams apart and gave them a boldness of spirit missing in most foes. "We used to tell each other to pull off the unexpected," jokes coach Orville Mitchell. "Shit on home plate."

Year after year, callow Maritimers sacrificed their summers, prodded by a zest for competition and a quest for some manner of public recognition. Saint Mary's University history professor Colin Howell, who has researched the effect of baseball on the community, writes that often the ballplayer settled and raised a family in the small town in which he starred. "The kind of status that you have in the community may result to some extent in you staying there because your [small-town fame] is not portable. Where do you take your reputation? It's the big-fish-in-a-small-pond phenomenon."

Certainly, athletes were not lured by money. Amateur teams were banned from paying players outright—although a few players, especially pitchers, were slipped $25 a week, and most starters received partial compensation for lost income when games took them away from their jobs. The Yarmouth Gateways, one of the best Nova Scotian senior teams of the era, would compensate employers to enable them to hire temporary staff until ballplayers returned to work. Other times, an athlete would find a couple of dollars in meal money stuffed into his pocket.

"One year the athletic association had a surplus, and we all got a Christmas card with $10 in it," says Yarmouth's Halley Horton. "My God, I kept that for the longest while. It was an appreciation."

"With us," recalls Liverpool Larruper pitcher Laurie Thorborne, "most of us would come off work that morning, drive to another town, play ball, maybe a double-header, then go back to work after the game."

If players played for joy, owners owned for reasons unclear. To lose a few hundred dollars was considered a good year for backers of ball teams in the Depression, and to break even was a remarkable accomplishment. Predictably, ownership changed regularly. Sometimes owners were well respected around town, sometimes not.

While most teams operated haphazardly, St. Stephen's was an exception. Prominent citizens—first a wealthy young businessman, then a clergyman, then a civil servant—scrutinized the bottom line and charted the team's ascension. "It was a dressed-up version," says pitcher Jim Morell, who played for several teams before joining the St. Stephen club. "It was just like the old Toronto Maple Leafs—tie and tails."

◆　◆　◆　◆

The major sources used for this book were personal interviews and newspapers. Both afforded rich harvests of information and amusement, only some of it intended.

The ballplayers, coaches and others who became my interview subjects were largely aged 75 to 85, and were eager to reminisce. I conducted most of the interviews during the summer of 1988, in Yarmouth, Liverpool, Halifax and Springhill in Nova Scotia, and in Saint John, Fredericton and St. Stephen in New Brunswick.

Since those interviews, several of the key men featured in this book, and who are quoted in the present tense, have passed away. Among them are second baseman Phil (Sweet Pea) McCarroll and outfielder Earl (Squirrelly) Ross, both of St. Stephen, and Doug Horton, of Yarmouth. However, most of the others with whom I met are in remarkably good health.

The St. Stephen interview sessions enhanced basic information I had gathered from 1978 to 1981 while working as a reporter for St.

Stephen's bi-weekly newspaper, the *Saint Croix Courier*. In total, the interviews produced more than 70 hours of tape recordings—and several quirky moments.

Without warning, inanimate objects became props in elaborate re-creations of past triumphs. Suddenly, an apple was a ball, a lamp or a cane was a bat, and living-room furniture was shoved aside to show the full extent of a pitcher's wind-up. Interestingly, several interviewees used the present tense when referring to former teammates. "He has a real problem running the bases," noted one. Understandably. "He" had been dead for more than 20 years! Another oddity was the high degree of animosity towards certain teammates. Of the four major teams featured in this work, all have at least one standing feud within their elderly brotherhood.

This aside, the extent and accuracy of recall was remarkable. An exact batting order, an umpire's disputed call, the number of spectators, the color of an opponent's hair, the expression on his face, the weather—all were just a query away. Memorized scores differed only slightly—if at all—from newspaper records.

The newspapers I used most were the *Saint Croix Courier*, the Saint John *Telegraph-Journal*, the *Halifax Herald* and the *Halifax Chronicle*. More than 3,000 articles were photocopied, dated and filed. Most of the articles originated on the sports pages.

Like virtually all sports journalism of the era, Maritime sports reporting was amusing, puzzling and uneven. Generally flawed in content, method and style, baseball reports were often overwritten, parochial and littered with jargon. This jargon helped ritualize the sport and seemingly placed the writer within the ballplayers' fraternity. Back then, few wrestled with the idea of a symbiosis between sportswriter and athlete. "I got along with all of [the players] because I wasn't much of a critic," says Ace Foley, who served as *Halifax Chronicle* sports editor for many years. "When we used to go on trips, I used to give them tips."

Nevertheless, newspapers were the media of record and the most influential vehicles of public information. (Radio was not yet as pervasive as the printed word.) For the young amateur athlete, the sports page provided public recognition—the ultimate reward for his sacrifice.

The Maritime press of the 1930s accorded baseball wide coverage. By mid-season, headlines commonly extended the width of the page, and come the playoffs, amateur baseball was often front-page news. The prestige of the Maritime finals—partially bestowed by the newspapers themselves—provided an excuse for perhaps the sportwriter's only trip that year. To justify expenses, reporters produced reams of copy. No detail was too trivial, and no trivia went undetailed for the overworked and underpaid reporter. "I was workin' seven days a week," says Foley. "Not only that, if two or three people were sick, I did their jobs, too. You never got an extra nickel for it. And when the Depression came, they cut salaries to $10 a week."

Extensive press coverage fuelled baseball's popularity, but other factors contributed as well. One of them was basic: players were neighbors and relatives. Their accomplishments generated a familial pride, while the team courted communal involvement. "In the small town," New Brunswick journalist David Folster wrote in a 1968 issue of the *Atlantic Advocate*, "the lowly fan has status. He's more than a face in the crowd. He's a part-time manager, adviser, ballpark builder, concessionaire, batting practice pitcher, ticket-taker, almost whatever he chooses. In short, he participates."

In the 1930s, there were also fewer distractions. What activities there were pulled people out of the house, to a fair, a bingo or a ball game. In addition, people travelled less. Poorer roads, fewer cars, annual vacations that lasted just one week, and a six-day work week all locked people to the home front.

In St. Stephen, the enticement of a winning team was an additional factor in drawing people to the ball diamond. Game crowds regularly exceeded 20 percent of the town's population, and playoffs frequently drew 75 percent. Other towns in the Maritimes could make similar claims at some point during the decade. Across the region, writes historian Colin Howell, baseball had become a unifying enthusiasm "that bridged class divisions and encouraged community solidarity." Indeed, baseball mattered.

"They used to say," recalls Foley, "that if a man had $100, he'd spend $50 on sports, $20 on drinks and the rest on his family."

Finally, two points about my approach in writing this book.

First, this work has a male gaze. Women in these pages are often portrayed as counterpoints, conquests and curiosities. This reflects the attitudes of the main characters and of the era. For women, it was a time when the economic and social doors kicked open at the turn of the century were slammed shut. Great Depression ideology insisted that women sacrifice personal ambitions to raise children, cook meals, wash clothes and, in many instances, struggle to feed a family of five on 80 cents a week. Women were generally not community leaders. Very rarely were they ballplayers.

Second, information already made public about Maritime amateur baseball is skeletal and candy-coated. The St. Stephen team and its era warrant a more comprehensive and honest assessment of the lost tapestries of friendship, community, sportsmanship and courage found in a team, a town and a time.

◆ 1 9 3 0 ◆
THE ONE THAT GOT AWAY

"If baseball championships are to be won by the use of the telephone, there seems to be little need of the expense of playdowns."
—Whidden Ganong and Bill Whitlock—

I N A TOWN where sports often seemed a social prerequisite, Roy Boles was almost somebody. He played hockey well and played baseball even better, and soon people in St. Stephen, New Brunswick, were starting to know him, appreciate him and treat him as if he were special. Strangers on the street greeted him with smiles and nods of approval, calling him by his first name, offering him status. It was all very seductive for a man in his early 20s.

So leaving town at the beginning of 1930 was tough. But it was the right thing to do. He was, after all, a married man—the head of the house, the breadwinner—and a man has to go where the jobs are. And in early 1930 a job awaited Boles in an Esso service station in Moncton, 150 miles to the east. So, in winter's nadir with talk of troubled times swirling, the ballplayer and his bride left town, perhaps for good. It was hard to say.

Losing a young ballplayer hurt a little, but for St. Stephen it was just the first in a sorry series of events that year.

Early one January morning, St. Stephen awoke to an orange sky. Flames that had ignited in one of the town's oldest buildings were by dawn Sunday sweeping through a succession of two-storey wooden structures. Five fire departments battled the infernos of indeterminable course and undeniable whim that caused $200,000 in damages to 13 businesses and their stocks. Lifelong investments were wiped out. Livelihoods vanished. Three families were left homeless.

At mid-afternoon, pockets of employees stood silently beneath a dome of smoke and steam and watched water play on charred ruins. Just 12 days into the decade, the town's commercial soul was gutted. Yet there was no panic. The people would rebuild, just as they had after the fire of 1889 and after every disaster before that. St. Stephen, you see, could cope.

Three months later, however, the knife twisted again and inflicted a deeper emotional wound.

Friday, March 28, produced a warm spring night, and St. Stephen's streets were lit and populated. At approximately nine o'clock, Rachael Boles, a 24-year-old maid of flawless repute, emerged from the back seat of a car and waved cheerfully to her two friends, a young woman and a young man. She had just enjoyed seeing Douglas Fairbanks, Sr., win girl and game in the movie *The Forward Pass*, and Rachael appeared in good spirits. She began the five-minute walk home from downtown, taking a widely used shortcut on a well-worn path.

A shy woman whose short, dark hair clung to her cherubic face, Rachael had been in need of a pleasant evening. She had recently spent a week with her ailing mother, and the visit had disturbed the dutiful daughter. In any case, Rachael herself seemed in general ill health. So when word sifted through town that she had disappeared, most assumed the sad young woman had taken her own life. Certainly, the notes found in her room suggested an eerie finality: "Give this to Greg, Sis. PS: As a keepsake from me."

It all seemed so neat, so obvious. Too obvious, some thought. Then, slowly, the doubting started.

First, the notes were explained away. Her friends told police that Rachael frequently left reminders to herself. But then came some unnerving information. Neighbors claimed to have heard, around midnight on the night Rachael had disappeared, the wrenching screams of a girl in agony. One neighbor had run from his house in time to see a car speeding away along the riverside. Soon, people began recalling that just last year a local businessman had been killed in Rachael's neighborhood—and the murderer was still at large! The mass imagination was in overdrive, and rumor fed off rumor. For weeks, few women and girls ventured out after dark.

"She has vanished completely as though the earth has swallowed her, leaving not a trace by which provincial and local police can trace her movements since that hour," reported St. Stephen's newspaper, the *Saint Croix Courier.* "This is the most baffling mystery the town has ever known."

Daily search parties of 40 men—including Rachael's father,

Stewart Boles—combed the surrounding woods. The St. Croix River was scoured, and an airplane hired from Saint John criss-crossed the river banks. Searchers examined train departure lists and nailed posters to telephone poles. Pressured and frustrated, St. Stephen town council offered a $500 reward for the discovery of Rachael's body. A couple of clairvoyants even emerged. One, known as the Mystery Man of Belfast, Maine, wrote Mr. Boles insisting that Rachael was floating in the St. Croix River, below St. Stephen on the Canadian side. She had taken her own life, the Mystery Man claimed, and the body would be found soon.

In early May, Rachael's bloated body was found lying face down, 30 feet above the high-water mark on a beach about 15 miles from St. Stephen on the American side of the river. Authorities said the two slight cuts on her forehead and cheek were likely results of the body banging into objects in the river. There were no abrasions on her body and no signs of violence. Death by drowning, they said. A suicide.

Nonetheless, many still had doubts. But it was spring, and this burned-out, traumatized little border town had reached its limits. So St. Stephen quietly buried Rachael and the mystery—the latter understood only by the river.

◆   ◆   ◆   ◆

The St. Croix River is a jagged 75-mile body—rising in the Chiputneticook Lakes and flowing northeasterly to Passamaquoddy Bay. At its mouth it severs Calais, Maine, and St. Stephen, New Brunswick.

For St. Stephen, the river is seminal. It is a reason for the town's birth and a symbol of its rejuvenation. French explorer Pierre Du Gua de Monts came upon the river in 1604, and with Samuel de Champlain and 80 others, he spent the pitiless winter on the Ile de Ste-Croix, approximately 10 miles down river from St. Stephen. Before spring, nearly half of the settlers died of scurvy. The remainder moved immediately to the more congenial climate of Port-Royal, in what is now Nova Scotia.

Eventually, in the wake of the American Revolution, British Empire Loyalists came to St. Stephen. Attracted by abundant forests and by the river itself, they settled the eastern bank of the river in 1784. Approximately 100 Loyalists made camp, and the mother country granted tools, rations and 100 acres for each family.

Allegedly, the town was named after a raucous member of a survey party. The word "saint," some historians insist, was added facetiously. Nevertheless, by 1790, with a population of several hundred, St. Stephen had grown into a busy lumbering centre with seven saw mills. The first schooner was built in 1797. King's Mast Road, the straight, sloping mile-long main street, accommodated the movement of king masts (pine trees three feet in diameter) down to the river.

Meanwhile, across the St. Croix River, in Calais, Maine, permanent settlers had arrived in 1770. In 1809 Calais was given its city charter, establishing itself rapidly as the area's shopping centre. During the War of 1812, the precarious juxtaposition of Calais and St. Stephen, which by now had strong economic and familial bonds, precipitated an agreement that neither community would take up arms. Still, peace required heroics by a courageous Methodist pastor from St. Stephen, Duncan McColl. McColl first dissuaded American soldiers, who had interrupted one of his sermons, from attacking St. Stephen. Subsequently, he pleaded successfully with British soldiers intent on spilling American blood in Calais. The British commander, after some thought, reportedly dubbed local residents a "queer" lot who would be virtually valueless on the battlefield. The British troops left quietly. Shortly after the War of 1812, St. Stephen loaned Calais some gunpowder for Fourth of July celebrations, thereby hatching the valley's favorite anecdote.

The mid-1800s were a time of affluence for St. Stephen, but by the late 1800s the forests were depleted and shipbuilding had declined. So the town switched its economic base to manufacturing. By 1900 the community of 2,800 inhabitants had two beverage and bottling companies, a shoe factory, a carriage factory, an axe factory, a soap manufacturer and a candy factory. Milltown, an adjoining community of 2,000 situated at the head of the tide water, had a cotton mill.

With few exceptions, this robust and diverse economy still existed in the 1930s. The mill, owned by Canada Cottons Ltd., had 500 automatic looms and employed 700. No Maritime town was better off, certainly none was more resilient—or more clannish. In 1930, St. Stephen mayor David R. Wilson actually boasted that the community featured a vast collection of "secret societies": the Masonic Lodge, the Oddfellows, the Knights of Pythias, the

Knights of Columbus, the Red Men, the Eastern Star, the Rebekah Lodge, the Pythian Sisters, the Orangemen and, soon, the Kiwanis.

Ninety-five percent British, the town gained comfort from ceremony, especially when ceremony was associated with the monarchy. (The 1937 coronation of George VI, for example, filled the streets.) This strong ancestral tie fed an appreciation of town history. A memorial park and a monument to the lost of the First World War sat near the main thoroughfare. Virtually everyone in St. Stephen knew that the library had been a boarding house for women who had worked in the candy factory, and that the town's oldest building, the Stone House, had accommodated British officers in the 1700s.

One of the few structures on Water Street to escape damage during the January 1930 fire was the Johnson Building, a sturdy brick edifice. Days before the fire, it had been selected to house a new sports-oriented community organization called the Mohawk Amateur Athletic Club. The Mohawk club melded St. Stephen's well-to-do and its middle class for bingos, card games and other fund-raising events in support of the tennis, curling, hockey, basketball and baseball teams it sponsored.

◆ ◆ ◆ ◆

Baseball. In the St. Stephen area the sport had special status. As early as the 1870s a team from the St. Croix Valley challenged teams from Saint John and Fredericton. There is pictorial record of a girls' baseball team in the 1890s in Bocabec, about 20 miles outside St. Stephen, and several recreational men's clubs played at the turn of the century. In 1913 a St. Stephen-Calais entry in the four-team Class D New Brunswick and Maine League drew boisterous crowds from throughout the valley, but the league folded after just one year.

In the 1920s, before large crowds, semi-professional teams from the four border towns—St. Stephen; Calais; Milltown, New Brunswick; and Milltown, Maine—gave furious exhibitions as the St. Croix Baseball League. By this time, the significant public opposition to professional baseball—which held that it would corrupt the manly virtues of courage, strength, teamwork and foresight found in the amateur game—had subsided. The border was ready to embrace the pros.

The St. Croix Baseball League featured high spirits, high spikes, and the spitball as an art form. Its feral hue mirrored the conviction that each community was distinct, nay, just a little superior. In the end, however, team managers were baseball men, not bookkeepers, and revenues seldom matched expenditures, no matter how hefty the gate receipts. Finally, when the money vanished, so did the four-year-old league. A few orphaned players landed spots with lesser teams in larger towns, but many stayed on the border, conceding that their glory days were over. It was these remaining players whom the Mohawk club sought for its new ball team: Orville Mitchell, Aubrey (Baldy) Moffatt, Raymond Jellison, George Purcell and Ike Vanstone. Yet the team's initial success was largely due to a name that never appeared on a line-up card—Ganong.

Opened 41 years earlier as a small bakery and sweets shop, Ganong Bros. was by 1917 the largest candy manufacturer in Canada. The family could also boast a long line of professionals and politicians. But young Whidden Ganong was interested in none of that in the late 1920s. He had a sense of adventure—his father, Arthur, vetoed a plan to join the horse artillery in India—and a penchant for baseball.

(Accompanied by a handsome scalawag named Bill Whitlock, Whidden once watched a ball game in St. Stephen one Saturday evening, then jumped in his Ford Roadster at 9 p.m. and bumped and twisted the 500 or more miles to Boston. He arrived, watched a Braves double-header that afternoon, then raced his car back to St. Stephen, reaching home early Monday morning.)

Whidden and Bill Whitlock, a businessman and sports promoter, were part of a small cadre of successful young men whose community consciousness was manifested largely in amateur athletics. Loaded with good intentions, they expounded an idealism that seemed naive even in less cynical times.

"Sometimes I feel that we all overlook the sacrifices that a purely amateur player makes when he gives of his time three or four nights a week for practices, with the added hazard of injury to himself," Whitlock once said in a speech. "Instead of finding fault with him, and razzin' him, if we would only give him an extra cheer and word of encouragement, it would not only be what he rightly deserves, but would make him feel that the fans were at least behind him, and he would work that much harder. For, after all, he is out there working his head off to win, while his only reward is to please the fans and place his home team as a winner on the sporting map."

That year, St. Stephen's Mohawk club entered a team named the Mohawks in the York-Charlotte Baseball League, a southwestern New Brunswick circuit with great expectations and four teams. The Mohawk uniform was not really one at all: a large, dark "M" was sewn haphazardly on the front of white sweatshirts, while pants, shoes and caps had been pilfered from earlier ensembles. Other teams were only slightly more dapper.

The Fredericton Imperials, based in the provincial capital of 20,000, were probably favored to win that season despite being little more than an amalgam of university students, men born in the last century and uninspired management. McAdam, a railway town of 3,000 approximately 40 miles north of St. Stephen, was a provincial hotbed for the Ku Klux Klan, and it hosted at least one major cross-burning ceremony in the late 1920s. Its baseball team was mediocre. The fourth team in the league was from Devon, a working-class afterthought of affluent Fredericton. Devon boasted several experienced players, notably Vince Shields—a Fredericton-born, part native Indian for whom the York-Charlotte league must have seemed like baseball purgatory.

Vincent William Shields could command a baseball like few men in the nation. A right-handed, submarine (nearly underhand) pitcher who had played semi-professionally in the 1920s with St. Stephen in the old St. Croix Baseball League, Shields carried a solid 185 pounds on a broad-shouldered, five-foot-11-inch frame. To supplement his pitching income and to await The Big Break, he worked in a St. Stephen garage, doing some wilderness guiding on the side. Those in the know insisted he had major league stuff, and Shields agreed. His was a bold dream in small-town Canada, but Shields was as confident as he was talented. By age 23, late in 1924, he was in the uniform of the National League's St. Louis Cardinals.

It was not a banner season for the Cards or for manager Branch Rickey, who would help Jackie Robinson shatter baseball's color barrier more than two decades later. St. Louis finished sixth in the eight-team league, 28-1/2 games behind the New York Giants. But at least the team had the great Rogers Hornsby to play second base and hit .424. They also had—for two glorious games—Vince Shields, who won one and lost one. In all, he pitched 12 major league innings, yielded 10 hits, walked three and struck out four, including an American icon named Casey Stengel. His earned-run average was 3.00. Shields had two hits in five at-bats, no doubt making him Canada's only .400 major league hitter.

The Cardinals were impressed with Shields and invited him to their spring training camp in 1925. Shields, however, lived in the real world and understood the caprice of the major leagues, where salaries were good but not great, and certainly not good enough to retire on. After the 1924 season he travelled to Detroit and worked in a Ford automobile factory. Aware of Shields' athletic prowess, Ford offered him $100 a game to pitch for the company team in Detroit's prestigious industrial league. Shields accepted and stayed for approximately five years, never again pitching in the big leagues.

By 1930, Vince Shields, a tired 29, had returned to New Brunswick and was playing for free for Devon in the York-Charlotte league. There, God-awful amateurs in hand-me-down uniforms pounded his once-unhittable fastball around dusty diamonds. His team finished last.

◆　◆　◆　◆

St. Stephen was easily the best team in the York-Charlotte league, winning 16 of 25 games. By placing first, they qualified to face defending New Brunswick champions Moncton Cercle Catholique de la Jeunesse Acadienne in the provincial semi-finals.

Under a brilliant late-August sun, the best-of-five series opened with Moncton winning a double-header, 10-8 and 9-0. The next day, the series shifted to St. Stephen's town-owned baseball facility—a grey, grassless expanse without dugouts, lighting, proper drainage or outfield fences. The clay surface required little maintenance—a heavy wooden scraper affixed to the back of a truck sufficed—and it rewarded infielders with true bounces on ground balls, moving as if they had been shot from a rifle. Many of the opponents pampered with grass infields at home feigned illness rather than stand under the sun and dodge white bullets for two hours on that skin diamond. Equally perilous was the flag pole—in deep centre field! No picnic either was right field, where a blinding early-afternoon sun caused many fielders to play by ear. Mud smeared under the eyes helped combat the glare a little.

The bleachers held 500, more than most Maritime ball fields of the day. Spectators could alternate their attention between the game and events on a half-mile horse-race track situated near the diamond's eastern entrance. There is considerable question whether the race track or the ball diamond came first. Whichever, it was a blissful marriage. "Sometimes, people would be watching the ball game, then suddenly move over and watch the horse race. When that was over, they'd come back over," says Mohawk outfielder George Purcell. The thick forest beyond the race track became a repository for outfielders' gloves between innings. The Mohawks' home had, as they say, character.

◆ ◆ ◆ ◆

Gloom blanketed the park that August as the Mohawks and Moncton CCs warmed up for the third game of the provincial semi-final series. The home side was down 2-0 in games to the reigning champions, and spectators knew that St. Stephen's pitching in Moncton had been horrid. And now the Mohawks' pitching corps was reduced to Howdy Clark.

His large head, round face, and ears that protruded like rearview mirrors all seemed designed for another man's body. Certainly, they did not belong on Howdy Clark's spindly frame. It was, nevertheless, an athlete's body and sometimes it served him well.

Although he threw right-handed, Clark had a southpaw's awkward delivery. He used a sidearm, looping motion that delivered a slow, inviting ball to home plate. It was straight and accurate, but without much spin the ball had a dead feeling when struck with a bat. As a result, few hits made it into the deep outfield. It became known as Howdy's Nothin' Ball, an appellation left undisputed by his catcher, Theo (Muddy) McLain, a burly American who would thrust his moistened finger into the air and announce, "There's a wind today. Howdy might have a curve."

What few opponents knew, however, was that the Nothin' Ball stemmed from a special clandestine lubrication. Not of the ball, but of Clark.

"He was drinkin' rye whiskey, straight," says Mohawk captain Orville Mitchell. "He just took a couple of nips out of it between innings and put it away. Somebody would stand behind the bench and hold it for him. About every inning or every two innings, he'd come in and have a little belt out of that pint. All the fans knew the history of Howdy, because it was common talk around town. Howdy had to have his tea."

Frequently, this magic elixir was supplied by team management, and usually by Bill Whitlock. Management realized that, with Clark, booze and baseball went hand-in-hand. Clark believed firmly that alcohol was responsible for his endurance and excellent control, so a pre-game pint for Clark was, well, an investment.

Once, in Moncton, outfielder George Purcell asked Whitlock for 50 cents for movie fare. "We can't waste money like that," Whitlock shot back. A few moments later, Clark approached Whitlock. "I know where I can get a bottle for $3," he said. Without hesitating, Whitlock reached inside of his pocket and handed Clark the money. "You son of a sea cook," Purcell exclaimed in an outburst about as close to swearing as he ever got. "You wouldn't give me 50 cents, but you just gave him $3 for a pint!" Whitlock smiled. "Yeah, but I know that I'm gonna get some of that pint."

By the time he was in his 30s, Clark was a town *flaneur* whose favorite drink was the next one and whose life was fuelled by nothing in particular. Married? Employed? Sort of. His whole existence seemed slightly out of focus. "He'd be out half the night," remembers Purcell, who roomed with Clark when the team travelled. "One time Howdy'd been drinkin', and he was feelin' pretty bad. We went to bed, but soon Howdy said, 'Get me somethin' to drink.' Well, I didn't know what to do. I never took a drink in my life. So I got up out of bed and reached over and turned on the tap and got a glass of water. He said, 'Don't be crazy. Pour that down the sink.' He was insulted, I guess."

During one road trip in Nova Scotia, Clark and his close pal, Earl (Squirrelly) Ross, by then a St. Stephen outfielder, persuaded a young woman to allow them to escort her home. "We was talkin' and this guy comes to the door and says, 'You scram!'" says Ross. "I said, 'You go to hell!' She said, 'That's my husband!' I ran out through the door—right through the door. But Howdy, he wanted to go back."

Having hit age 30, Clark's best pitching years—if there had been any *best* years—were well behind him at the outset of St. Stephen's dynasty. However, he did give some strong performances, notably one wonderful afternoon against McAdam when he threw nine hitless innings. Sometimes, he even pitched without booze. It was after one of those dry games near the end of his career that St. Stephen's renowned centre fielder and teatotaller, Gordon Coffey, approached him.

Coffey moved in close and stared Clark in the eye. "You can pitch all right without that bottle of gin, can't you?"

Clark stopped, glanced away for a moment, then flashed a wide grin. "Yeah," he said. "I fooled them for a long time, didn't I?"

♦ ♦ ♦ ♦

So in game three of the 1930 New Brunswick semi-final, the team's fate rested with Clark. This time it was not misplaced. He surrendered eight hits, none of them in the final four innings, and beat Moncton's Roy Boles, the St. Stephen native who had left town early that year, 6-5. In game four, later that same day, Clark starred again. Although he gave up hit after hit, he won 8-6, tying the series. The game had been called after seven innings because of darkness.

In one day, Clark had pitched 16 consecutive innings, yielded 21 hits, struck out 14 and walked just one. It was the ultimate athletic accomplishment of his life. But after it was over, he accepted the congratulations of his teammates and quietly headed into the night to celebrate—alone.

That night St. Stephen crackled with excitement. To win would be wonderful, but to beat Moncton—the defending provincial champions who had lured away young Boles—would sweeten victory so.

Actually, just finishing the series would be a feat in itself. The deciding contest would be the fifth game in three days, and both teams were exhausted. Pitching reserves were at rock bottom. The CCs delegated veteran Phil LeBlanc to start, while the Mohawks called on an erratic and slow right-hander from Milltown, New Brunswick, Wilfred (Tot) Kilpatrick. "He was kind of a pitcher, of sorts," says Mohawk captain Orville Mitchell.

In game five, the CCs struck quickly, scoring twice in the first inning. The Mohawks countered, and heading into the final inning, it was tied 4-4. Kilpatrick blanked Moncton in the top of the ninth before 1,200 fans as an arsenal of cowbells echoed off nearby hills. "Excitement was at a fever pitch," reported the *Saint Croix Courier*.

As the home team came to bat in the bottom of the ninth, the entire St. Croix Valley seemed to pause. The first two batters, Kilpatrick and right fielder Squirrelly Ross, went down easily. With two out and the bases empty, it all fell to veteran second baseman Orville Mitchell, the acting coach, the team captain and a former semi-pro. On the second pitch Mitchell drove the ball past Moncton's shortstop for a base hit, bringing up Harry Boles, the soft-spoken third baseman and older brother of Moncton's Roy Boles.

"Then the unexpected happened," said the *Courier.* "Boles drove what normally would have been a single through second, and the crack of the bat and the ball was to Mitchell what the pistol shot is to [Canadian Olympic sprinter] Percy Williams. Through second he tore while the field scrambled after the ball, over third in a flash and safely home with the winning run."

Teammates surged from the bench and fans ran onto the field to surround Mitchell and grasp his hand. Mitchell would have many other memorable moments, but none as spectacular as this brazen dash amid the cowbells. Shocked, the CCs quietly collected their equipment, slipped beneath the wave of joy and left the field.

◆ ◆ ◆ ◆

The first public hint of protest appeared within a week, in a short newspaper story in the Saint John *Telegraph-Journal.* The article speculated that the scheduled playoff game between the Saint Johns and the Mohawks could be ruled an exhibition game. St. Stephen management soon learned why.

Moncton had officially protested the series, claiming that the Mohawks had used ineligible players, specifically two Americans: catcher Muddy McLain and infielder Aubrey (Baldy) Moffatt, the latter born in Milltown but living across the St. Croix River in Calais, Maine. The matter reached the desk of T. R. Loudon, president of the Amateur Athletic Union of Canada, who ruled that no American residing in the United States was eligible to play for a Canadian team in Canada. With uncharacteristic dispatch, the Maritime Provinces Branch of the Amateur Athletic Union of Canada agreed that McLain and Moffatt were ineligible. It promptly ordered the series replayed, beginning in Moncton.

In this year of disasters, St. Stephen buckled under one more blow. Before Mohawk management could formally respond to the athletic union's decree, the Mohawk players met and decided not to return to Moncton. Had not the series been won fairly? Had the spirit of friendly competition evaporated completely? It was a matter of principle. And money. To go back would cost $100, and resources were scant. There was little choice: the series was forfeited.

"A large crowd was on hand for [game one of the replay]," reported the *Daily Times* of Moncton, "and although it had been rumored that the Mohawks would not put in a second appearance nothing definite was heard from the tribesmen's camp, and arrangements for the game were gone ahead with. It was an irate gathering of faithful who sat, hunched and cold on the windswept bleachers awaiting the arrival of the Mohawks who never appeared."

Protests were common during baseball playoffs, and the sport was diminished because of it. But the press was especially indignant about this seeming injustice. The *Saint Croix Courier* ran a front-page story that was headlined, "The Amateur Baseball Farce." *Telegraph-Journal* columnist Louis McKenna wrote: "Another chapter in the greatest of all farces, the New Brunswick baseball playoff round, was written Saturday when the St. Stephen Mohawks did not show up in Moncton ... The Moncton squad, a team that proved to be weaker than the border aggregation, will meet Campbellton for the mythical and cloudy New Brunswick championship." Even Moncton's *Daily Times* conceded that provincial baseball had been given "a black eye."

Three points propelled the outcry. First, Moncton pitcher Boles had played for the make-shift St. Stephen Ravens in 1929. He was never released from that team and was still technically bound to play in St. Stephen. The Amateur Athletic Union of Canada deemed Boles ineligible and suspended him, as it did Moffatt and McLain. (Boles nevertheless played for Moncton in the Maritime finals, which were won by Halifax.) Second, said the critics, the Maritime branch of the athletic union, under Monctonian Charles C. Gillespie, had mishandled the protest. The branch deferred the matter to the Amateur Athletic Union of Canada, even though the branch's by-laws said that such protests must be handled at the local level. The third and perhaps most acrid point was that everyone had ignored the gentlemen's agreement permitting teams to use players from neighboring towns. Particularly troubled by this final point was Mohawk club president Whidden Ganong.

Ganong confronted the athletic union's annual meeting that October, asserting that St. Stephen and Calais were fundamentally one town. They shared water, electricity, gas, fire departments, street cars, a curling rink, a bowling alley, a country club, employment, schooling and even romance, he said. Indeed, hardly a family had not married into the other side, somewhere down the line. "It can be seen that only the international boundary prevents the places from being one town," Ganong said. The residence rule, stating that Calais athletes could move temporarily to St. Stephen and be deemed eligible, was merely technical niggling and an inconvenience to the players, he said.

Ganong and Bill Whitlock also sent a scathing letter to the *Courier.* Its thrust: playoffs seemed unnecessary when having elected officials in the baseball association was the apparent road to the championship. "If baseball championships are to be won by the use of the telephone, there seems to be little need of the expense of playdowns," they wrote.

Interestingly, during most of the 1930s the Maritime branch of the athletic union would be headed by two St. Stephen men: first William Webber and then Whitlock. Eligibility of American players was never again an issue.

◆ 1 9 3 1 ◆
THE CLIMB TO NUMBER ONE

"Get the hell back where you belong!"
—Tush Foley—

A S THE NATION winced beneath high unemployment, long food lines and personal tragedies, St. Stephen's economic spirits remained high. Automobile sales were up 15 to 30 percent over 1929. The rayon division of the Milltown cotton mill was working day and night, 100 looms spinning, 60 more girls needed. At Ganong Bros. chocolate factory, reputation and sales grew steadily. The Town of St. Stephen hired 50 extra men for street work. Ironically, even the fire of 1930 that had gutted the downtown sparked a local building boom.

About the only failure was the Worley Water Waver, a stillborn brainchild of a St. Stephen husband-and-wife chiropractic team. The invention was supposed to alleviate back pain and make the Worleys rich and famous gilding-the-lily chiropractors. They spent a full year travelling and trying to hustle the contraption, but by 1931 the Worley Water Waver had sunk into the great tub of failed genius. The couple quietly returned home and reopened their practice.

St. Stephen fed off a balanced diet of hard work and trivial distraction, the latter receiving ample coverage in the local newspaper. People flocked to talking pictures with teasing titles such as *Let Us Be Gay*, *Misbehaving Ladies*, *Caught Cheating*, and *The Lady Who Dared*. More than 100 stood wide-eyed as a 12-passenger amphibian aircraft with "comfortable chairs and wide windows" sat for 30 minutes at the Calais airport. Meanwhile, Cappy McWha was winning the provincial curling championship, and a local boy and his hens were setting the pace at the New Brunswick Egg Laying Contest. And every week at the Royal Canadian Legion, a couple of cooks named Fred served up clam chowder you could eat with a fork. On the border in 1931, hard times seemed a distant notion.

Among the prime beneficiaries of the town's comparative affluence was the Mohawk baseball team. Enough employment meant men could stay and play ball on the border. At least one player returned there to work. Roy Boles, who had left for Moncton in 1930, accepted a job in a St. Stephen garage. It was a significant reunion. Boles, a central figure in the Moncton-St. Stephen controversy the season before, was the competent pitcher the Mohawks lacked, and he would soon develop into one of the best amateur ballplayers in the country. Boles was also reunited with a brother four years his senior, the Mohawks' third baseman and most staid citizen, Harry Boles.

◆ ◆ ◆ ◆

Steady. Harry Boles learned to hate that word. To him it had come to mean unspectacular, mechanical, colorless, dull. Roy was the star pitcher. Harry was steady. Roy was a great hitter. Harry was consistent. Roy was special. Harry was ignored.

"Ever since I was a kid, I didn't like crowds," says Harry, called Dad by his teammates. "I still could never get up in front of a crowd and make a speech. I'd forget everything that I was supposed to say. But eventually it got that I could perform in front of crowds because I didn't have to say anything."

Besides, words sometimes got in the way.

Such as the time a bonny young woman caught the eye of the quiet, thin-featured fellow at that square dance in the big hotel on the wharf. He asked her to dance and she agreed and they moved about with utmost reserve until the music stopped and these tender strangers found they could not part because a button of his coat was entangled in the lace of her dress. So they stood there struggling to free her and giggling a little and trying to hide the fact that they were both turning a glowing crimson and ... then ... the young woman realized just how very, very handsome he was.

When Harry met Susan, there were never any doubts. Not then, and not after more than 60 years together, as the music still plays and she still remarks how very, very handsome he is.

To support a wife and a family, Boles found a decent, steady job with a lumber company, staying there for 48 years. In the summers he played senior baseball, the only man in the St. Croix Valley to do so from 1930 to 1939. Local member of Parliament Burton Hill rewarded Boles' service with an all-expenses-paid trip to see the World Series in Yankee Stadium in 1936.

"He played the same every day," says teammate Jim Morell. "I never saw a third baseman like him. He would throw a strike over there every time. He never made any spectacular plays, but he never made any bad ones."

Despite his colorlessness, Harry Boles had a loyal following. During one batting practice, Gordon Coffey moved over to Boles' young son, Bob, who was watching near the screen.

"Who's that old fella out there?" Coffey inquired.

"That's my dad," chirped Bob.

"Oh yeah?"

"Yeah. And you know what else?"

"What?" asked Coffey.

"He can lick any man in the world."

◆　◆　◆　◆

New to the St. Stephen Mohawks in 1931 was the coach, Arthur Middlemiss. The friendly candy maker was a pudgy, regular guy in his 40s, wise enough to realize that most of the team knew more about baseball than he did. His idea of strategy was to stand on the sidelines, hands resting on his stomach, and shout, "Let's go, gang. OK, boys. Watch out this inning. We're gonna hit this inning." Interestingly, in a brief profile the *Saint Croix Courier* called Middlemiss "the mind behind the team," bestowing on him "the lion's share of the credit" for the team's success. The fact that players did not protest such a distortion is sound testimony to the personal regard they had for the well-meaning Middlemiss.

Two others joined the team that season. Raymond Moffatt, a high-strung, combative native of Milltown, New Brunswick, was a good hitter and a deft fielder whose magnificent baseball instincts were repeatedly obscured by a festering mean streak. (An older and even more belligerent brother, Baldy, had played for the Mohawks in 1930.) The second addition was a slim, handsome schoolteacher destined to become the archetypal amateur centre fielder. Gordon Coffey, age 21, had played baseball in Fredericton the previous year, but that season was merely a footnote to what laid ahead in his home town.

Still simmering from the disqualification in last year's playoffs, the Mohawks were determined to use players from the American side of the St. Croix River. If not strictly allowed—the amateur associations were still vacillating—the team felt it morally correct to have Calais residents represent the community because as many as one in five fans of the club hailed from Calais. And furthermore, this regulatory aberration would enable St. Stephen to compete fairly with communities as much as 12 times larger. It seemed only sporting. After all, sportsmanship and gamesmanship were not mutually exclusive.

"We got smart," says captain Orville Mitchell. "In 1931, nobody said anything until we went into the playoffs. And we knew that we would get another holler from Moncton or Nova Scotia. We got rid of [infielder] Baldy Moffatt—we didn't need him—but we wanted [American catcher] Theo McLain. Theo and [Canadian outfielder] George Purcell were first cousins. We got one of the immigration officers to land Theo as an immigrant, and gave his residence as George Purcell's house. He used to stay there during the playoffs, but of course he was still working in the Calais post office. But after 1931 nothing really ever happened about using the Calais players."

Each year, St. Stephen became more adept at smuggling players. Ken Kallenberg, a teenaged pitcher from Calais who joined the team in mid-decade, would move in with a St. Stephen furniture salesman. "I used to go over in the spring and stay over at his place for probably a week," says Kallenberg. "Actually, all I'd do was to go over at night and sleep there and get up and have breakfast in the morning, then come back home."

With the desired Americans in tow, the Mohawks swept through the league, now called the York-Charlotte-Carleton Senior Baseball League, and into the provincial playdowns. Their opponents were the Saint John Martellos, champions of the truculent Saint John City League.

Beneath the historical ornaments—Canada's oldest incorporated city and refuge to hundreds of United Empire Loyalists—Saint John, New Brunswick, in the 1930s was an ignoble port of 40,000 possessing an unrelenting scroll of fog, a thick industrial crust and an unyielding grit. As a result, residents were simultaneously quarrelsome, warm and innovative. Saint Johners designed the first compound marine engine, erected the first steam fog whistle and helped invent the controllable-pitch airplane propeller. It was the birthplace of film magnate Louis B. Mayer and of actor Walter Pigeon, neither of whom exactly embraced their old home town. During the 1930s, it delivered actor Donald Sutherland, commenced the journalism career of native son Charles Lynch and became the base for the financial empire of a Presbyterian Scot named Kenneth Colin Irving. Still, New Brunswickers dubbed Saint John the armpit of the province, and it seemed constantly under siege. Its civic motto: *O, Fortunati, quorum jam moenia surgunt.* (Oh fortunate ones whose walls are now raised up.)

Baseball was Saint John's summer pastime, challenged only by bickering, which local ballplayers and coaches elevated to a science. And in 1931 no one out-bickered or outplayed the Martellos, who were captained by a 34-year-old legend named Charles Gorman, the Nonpareil.

◆ ◆ ◆ ◆

Private Charles Gorman, of the 140th Battalion, Machine Gun Division, a veteran of Vimy Ridge and Hill 70, lay suffering in a British hospital bed in September 1918. The German shrapnel lodged in his right thigh, the doctors said, would end his promising career as a competitive skater. Two months later, near Armistice Day, 20-year-old Gorman came home to Saint John. A former newspaper delivery boy who was poor and uneducated still, he was determined to prove the doctors wrong. And he did so in typically spectacular fashion.

Six years later, Gorman was an Olympic speedskater, beaten only by Clas Thunberg, of Finland. For the next two years the tenacious Gorman vowed revenge.

His chance came in January 1926 at the world speedskating championships on Lily Lake, a vast inner-city body near downtown Saint John. The city rocked with anticipation as the big day approached. "The committee in charge has made arrangements for the whistles of the city factories and the ships in the harbour to blow at 11 o'clock as an announcement that the races are on," reported the *Telegraph-Journal.* "All the foundries will join in."

Thunberg and American ace John O'Neil Farrell, of Chicago, were among the more than 30 competitors on hand, reportedly the best assemblage of skating talent ever. The championships comprised sprints—Gorman's specialty—and longer races. Unfortunately for Gorman, the title came down to the final event—a five-mile, 30-lap race with a field of 27, including the great distance man, Farrell. But the home-town favorite was confident, assuring the rink keeper just moments before the race that he was about to "win the fiver."

Initially, it appeared an idle boast. Gorman got off to a very slow start and at one point was last. With just a few laps to go he was far behind Farrell, who was skating with measured efficiency. Then, as 25,000 fans cheered and a snowy wind slapped his face, Gorman bent low and passed skater after skater until Farrell was in his sights. With one lap remaining, he caught and passed Farrell, slashing to the finish line as world champion. His time was 18 minutes, seven seconds.

Gorman immediately collapsed onto the ice, where he lay for several minutes, gasping for air. A newspaper reporter approached the exhausted hero and was quickly rebuffed. "All I want to do," wheezed the Nonpareil, "is get my clothes changed and go home and tell mother."

The quest enthralled his home town, which celebrated into the night and subsequently presented its hero with a gold watch. But in victory's immediate afterglow Gorman was remarkably composed. Following the race he had gone directly for a rubdown, then straight home. Only later that night did he venture out, to a dance.

"I can tell you," Gorman said a few days later, "after you win and look back on it, it doesn't seem so hard at all. It's when you lose that it all seems hard."

When he retired from speedskating in 1928, Gorman held seven indoor and outdoor world records, some of which outlasted the decade. He was also a good sprinter, an avid cyclist and a ballplayer who had been offered a professional contract at age 28. He declined and suited up instead with the Saint John Martellos, with whom his bellicose style mirrored Ty Cobb's. He relished this comparison to his idol—often called the most despised man ever to play the sport—and frequently displayed his own brand of hard-headedness. "Playing in Saint John one time," says Mohawk pitcher Roy Boles, "I hit Gorman on the top of the head and [the ball] bounced over the backstop. It made a sound, too! He was holdin' onto his head goin' to first base."

Years later, Martellos coach Aubrey Snodgrass recalled the time before a playoff game when Gorman came to him with a rather forceful suggestion. "He said, 'Aub, you better be smart today and let me lead off.' Well, to keep peace in the family, I said, 'OK.' He bunted the first ball down the third base line and was off like a streak. When they threw to first, he was not there. They threw to second. He was not there. They threw to third. He had just left. They threw to home plate but by that time he was complimenting me on my fine judgment in me letting him lead off." Gorman had turned what should have been a sacrifice out into an inside-the-park home run.

In the mid-1930s, Gorman, a bachelor, learned he had cancer of the lymph glands. He died in February 1940. A statue of him stands in the middle of Saint John.

◆ ◆ ◆ ◆

For Gorman and his Martellos, 11-2 losers in the first game of a best-of-three series, the 1931 New Brunswick semi-final had come down to a last-gasp, bottom-of-the-ninth challenge with runners on second and third, two outs and the score 6-5 for the Mohawks and pitcher Howdy Clark.

To the plate lumbered the Nonpareil, who had just one hit in four attempts in the game. He was overdue.

St. Stephen fans who had journeyed to Saint John baited the great athlete. As he stepped into the batter's box they chanted, "Million-dollar legs, 10-cent brain!" Still, their heckling was barely audible over the roar of 2,000 Martello supporters who spat back insults at Mohawk fans.

Clark, the Mohawks' master of the Nothin' Ball, seemed oblivious to the uproar. He exhibited his usual vacant expression as he peered in at the intense batsman, who by then must have been snorting steam. The first pitch was a ball. Gorman straightened up for a moment, then hunkered down once more, his powerful hands locked like vices around the bat handle. On the next pitch he swung from the heels and connected solidly. Martello fans sprang to their feet.

But Clark's pitch, dead and heavy, caused the ball to float meekly into an outfielder's glove for the final out of the game and of the series.

A few days later, in a letter to the editor of the *Saint Croix Courier*, an unidentified Mohawk player—possibly catcher Muddy McLain—took a final shot at Gorman. "The world of sport has no place for a squawker. A man or a team that can't take a licking without playing the baby is far better off out of it than in it. [Fans who] applaud every move of a ball player, getting by on laurels won in another branch of athletics, a man who plays constantly to the grandstand, who snarls and kicks rapidly on every decision made by an official and who finally changes a game of ball into a farcical succession of senseless disputes, would ruin the game in the best baseball town in the globe.... But we wonder how much longer Charles I. Gorman is going to get away with this stuff he's being pulling off for years.

"[In Saint John, Gorman] was playing a far different role from that of the jocular rather fat athlete trying to play ball ... that he had assumed in St. Stephen and was his old snarling self. His teammates followed his lead, kicking on called strikes against them that were right in the groove, flocking around the plate to protest every ruling and finally spoiling completely what might have been a pretty fair ball game.... So [St. Stephen umpire Tush] Foley kept his head and took whatever abuse he could stand from Gorman [showing] that while Charles I. might be getting away with murder he wasn't scaring anyone."

◆   ◆   ◆   ◆

Mohawk players and management had lived for 12 months with the ignominious conclusion of the 1930 season. The memory held fast of Moncton Cercle Catholique de la Jeunesse Acadienne's successful protest of St. Stephen's use of two American players, while knowing that they themselves were also using an ineligible player.

Atonement commenced on September 13, 1931, with the New Brunswick final. Roy Boles, now with St. Stephen, beat the CCs in game one and, later that day, pitched part of game two—a remarkable 12-inning, 2-1 Mohawk victory. However, the next day in Moncton, the CCs tied the series, savaging Clark 11-1 in game three, then in game four edged Boles, who was pitching his third game in 26 hours.

Both teams claimed the right to host the deciding game. After lengthy discussions, the Maritime branch of the national athletic union selected Moncton, stipulating that all of St. Stephen's expenses be paid through the game's receipts.

When the game opened the next weekend, Boles attacked his former mates with robot-like precision. Seemingly unaffected by a raw wind, he threw pitches that nibbled at the corners and caused Moncton batters to chase balls they had little chance of hitting. Meanwhile, the Mohawks slashed Moncton's pitching for three runs in the first inning, two in the sixth and two more in the seventh. Revenge was sweet—and it seemed astonishingly simple.

Up 7-0 as Moncton came to bat in the ninth inning, victory appeared certain. Then suddenly, St. Stephen's defence faltered.

Third baseman Harry Boles permitted a ball to pass between his legs. An error. Roy Boles walked the following batter, then surrendered a single to the next. A run crossed. As the press watched the Moncton fans change into "a rabid, fiercely yelling mob," the CCs were finally breaking through. But veteran Mohawk left fielder George Lee had other ideas.

When Moncton's Copie LeBlanc reached second on a hit to left, Lee spotted the ball a few yards away in the grass, but turned away in mock panic. "It's over there!" he instructed shortstop Rainnie Moffatt, while pointing away from the ball. "Get it, it's over there!" Moffatt obeyed but hesitated, then stopped, all adding to the illusion of confusion.

Seeing this, LeBlanc danced gingerly away from second base. Out of the corner of his eye Lee watched LeBlanc's progress, waiting until the runner had reached the point of no return. Suddenly, Lee did an about-face, scooped up the ball and relayed it to second base, where George Purcell tagged an embarrassed LeBlanc, the victim of a perfect ruse. Two out.

The Mohawks held off the remainder of the Moncton rally to win 7-5 and capture their first New Brunswick provincial championship. Atonement achieved. Time to celebrate.

"We decided to do a little hoot-owlin'," recalls Mohawk captain Orville Mitchell. "At about three o'clock in the morning we were right out front of the hotel, singin' and havin' a helluva good time. We weren't really drinkin' that much: we didn't have any money to buy much liquor. We were just singin' away, and then five o'clock came around. Finally, this cop came by. He said, 'Look boys, you won the championship, but the game's over. Now it's time to hit the hay. If you don't, I got a place for you downtown, and the beds aren't nearly as comfortable as those up there in The American House.' So we hit the sack. The cops were pretty understanding."

Predictably, Bill Whitlock and Howdy Clark were at the heart of the revelry, says Mitchell. He recalls that he had a pint of liquor stashed in his hotel room, saving it for later. But Whitlock and Clark snuck in to Mitchell's room, drank the bottle dry, then filled it with tea. The next morning Mitchell met them in the hallway and asked if they would like a little drink. "They said, 'Oh no, no, no. We couldn't touch it,'" Mitchell recalls. "After a while, I went back to the hotel room to get the bottle: I planned to treat somebody else. I didn't drink much of it—nothin' but god-damned tea! I heard them laughin' outside, and I laughed too. What else could I do?"

The Mohawks started for home buoyed by victory and a little sick from celebrating. Early that Sunday afternoon, about a mile from St. Stephen on the Gore Bridge, the team encountered more than 200 cars emitting a wall of noise that cracked the placid countryside. Joyous and bewildered, the players boarded a rented bus as a Calais marching band mustered behind. Cars filed in behind the band and the procession wound through the euphonious streets of St. Stephen, up into Milltown, across the bridge to Milltown, Maine, down through Calais, and finally back into St. Stephen. Hundreds of people stood along the route, cheering, waving handkerchiefs and reaching out to their misty-eyed heroes in an unbroken stream of appreciation.

"That was a big surprise," says Mitchell. "We really weren't looking for anything. In fact, we didn't know what to expect." The parade ended at a local restaurant where manager Bill Whitlock, coach Art Middlemiss, umpire Tush Foley and several venerable citizens spoke at length about athletic grandeur and town pride.

Then catcher Muddy McLain, who stuttered when he spoke, and outfielder Ike Vanstone, both tenors, sang a few numbers. Then the team was invited to another banquet, and then to an oyster supper. Then came the Westville Miners and the Maritime semi-finals.

Westville, Nova Scotia, had known wealth and glory. In 1866, coal was discovered in large quantity and soon the Intercolonial Coal Company developed land around the town. In the peak years around 1910, three companies worked the seams. But by 1931, this sullen community of 3,000 just off the Northumberland Strait had seen several mines close. Soon most shafts would shut down completely.

As the black hand of the Great Depression gripped Westville, baseball existed as one of the few things to exalt. The Westville Miners had won the 1928 Nova Scotia senior title, and in 1931 they dethroned the Halifax Casinos to become provincial champions once more.

Westville's ball diamond was a barren facility that sat atop coal deposits. Its surface once became so hot that players keeled over and had to be assisted off the field. The team benches sat out in the open, making players vulnerable to the sun and to spectators, who were prone to flick coal at the Miners' opponents. The Miners were important people around town, and betting reached $100 each for key games. Players benefited from the odd perk, several earning $2 or $3 a game during an era when a man slaved 12 hours for $1 and bought weekly room and board for $4. The team at one point imported a couple of Americans, but they arrived to chase skirts, not baseballs, and were soon sent packing. So the Westville Miners did it with local talent led by Billie Richardson, an intelligent, young southpaw with a good change of pace who had finished every game he had started that year.

On the last afternoon in September, Richardson finished his warm-up pitches and awaited the first St. Stephen Mohawk batter of the Maritime semi-finals.

"I said to myself, 'That left-hand pitcher isn't going to bother us a helluva lot,'" says Orville Mitchell. "[One early inning, lead-off hitter] Ike Vanstone and I were up there just waiting to go to the plate, and I said, 'Ike, you lay down a bunt along the third base line. I'll push you along. They'll be tongue-tied. They won't be expecting that.'

"Jeez, they never even made a play on him. I think he almost could have made second. Then I came up and I was supposed to sacrifice because of the reputation we'd heard about Richardson. I batted right and drew a walk. There we were, men on first and second, and Harry Boles comes up and hits a double over the shortstop's head. Ike scored; I landed on third. We got four runs in the inning, and Billie Richardson was history.

"Richardson had a kid of about 18 years old tryin' to catch him. And this kid was droppin' about every third ball. Then we said, no more bunting, now we'll steal. It was like walkin' around those bases. It would have broken the heart of a grindstone."

The Mohawks won that first game 12-4, then returned home to sweep the series with a 12-3 victory.

Now only the Charlottetown Abegweits, champions of Prince Edward Island, and two important decisions stood between the Mohawks and their first Maritime title. Decision one: the starting pitcher. That was easy. Roy Boles. Decision two: the umpire. That was easy, too. Tush Foley.

◆ ◆ ◆ ◆

During the playoffs, and especially during the Maritime final, teams arrived equipped with their own umpire, and the two umpires usually did a good job of alternating base-line and home-plate duties. Nevertheless, for reasons not entirely of their own making, umpires all over the Maritimes in the 1930s were punched, cursed, threatened, spat upon, impaled with hat pins and generally humiliated. (Once, in Cambridge, Nova Scotia, an umpire was arrested right on the field and charged with wife beating.) The press delighted in arbiter angst and helped perpetuate it with regular, scathing assessments.

"Handcuffed at the plate because of the worst case of barefaced robbery or gross incompetence on the part of the umpire," wrote the *Saint Croix Courier* about a St. Stephen loss, "the team was forced to swing at balls that were hitting the dirt and missing the plate by a least a foot.... The world's worst umpire in the person of Jack Doak was seeing more corners on the plate than there are in the Vatican."

To survive, umpires tended to be large men with booming voices and able right hooks. One was a curly-haired Saint Johner named Johnny Lifford, the Canadian middleweight boxing champion. A rugged lot, to be sure, but not always competent.

"Nowadays, you have to qualify, take a course and be graded," says Armond Wigglesworth, a journalist from Liverpool, Nova Scotia, who covered many 1930s Maritime finals. "But back then, just because you were an old catcher or an old ballplayer they thought it qualified you to call balls and strikes. They only had an umpire down first and a home plate umpire. Two people. You got some weird decisions down second and third. And some of those decisions were home-town decisions."

Being biased in favor of the home team was as old as Maritime baseball, which itself had existed since the mid-19th century. "After a game between the Saint John Nationals and the Halifax Socials in 1888," historian Colin Howell wrote in *Social History* in 1989, "the Saint John press charged umpire William Pickering, who regularly played second base with the Socials, with 'bare-faced cheating', and also alleged that a Mr. F. Robinson of Halifax had bribed the umpire. Robinson admitted bragging to friends in a local hotel that he had bought Pickering, but denied actually having done so."

Former *Halifax Chronicle* sports editor Ace Foley says that sometimes he would take umpires to task. "And in the car coming home, I'd say to him, 'You sure looked around today and saw what town you were in.' It was true. And he'd improve a bit—if he was a good umpire."

Nova Scotia's most ubiquitous umpire was actually a native of Milltown, New Brunswick, Frank (Peppah) Martin. (The Maine accent turned Pepp*er* to Pepp*ah*.) Martin once required a police escort to leave a game in Halifax, was punched by a player in Kentville, Nova Scotia, and had his face so swollen by a foul tip that he could not put his mask on for days. Yet he enjoyed the sport and often played to the crowd.

Yarmouth Gateways pitcher Nate Bain remembers: "I was fiddlin' around on the mound—it wasn't a very exciting game—and off comes Frank's mask, and he lets go a bellow and he comes walkin' out and starts pointin' at the slab. Then he leans over to me and says, 'Now watch the crowd.' And, sure enough, they are yellin', 'Get out of here, Martin.' Then he leans in again and says, 'This is really gonna get them goin'.' He started to point at me. I turn my back, and he starts followin' me around the mound, still pointin'. The crowd is really givin' it to him. Finally, he says to me, 'There, we have a game now. Thanks very much.'"

Tush Foley was Martin's counterpart in New Brunswick. A Calais native, Foley had massive shoulders, huge hands and a foreboding swagger that courted mayhem. He had a lasting love for baseball that vastly exceeded his ability to play it, however. So he umpired and formed not an entirely inept side known as Tush Foley's All-Stars, which played around the St. Croix Valley late in the decade.

He became a Maine State Highway patrolman with a clear-eyed, square-jawed, all-American view of justice. Once, at a prize fight in Rockland, Maine, Officer Foley, who was off duty at the time, hopped into the ring, pulled a disqualified fighter off the referee and ordered the angry pug back to his dressing room, or they— Foley and the fighter—would have a go at it right on the spot. The boxer left.

◆ ◆ ◆ ◆

The first two games of the best three-out-of-five Maritime final series were embarrassingly one-sided. In game one at the St. Stephen diamond, the Mohawks ran wild on Charlottetown's pitching in an error-filled 18-8 game. The next day, the Abbies committed nine more errors and lost 13-7 to Howdy Clark.

Spectators were surprised and, perhaps, slightly disappointed by the ease with which the Mohawks had dismissed the Island's best and taken a 2-0 lead in the series.

"St. Stephen fans got most of their enjoyment out of a terrific riding of the umpire-in-chief, Dr. Dugan [of Charlottetown]," J. Louis McKenna wrote in the Saint John *Evening Times-Globe.* "The climax came in the eighth when the Doc overruled Foley, base umpire, [and called a Charlottetown player] safe at third when he was caught off base. After a heated debate in which nearly all the players and both umpires took part, and during which Dugan threatened to call the game, the Mohawks agreed to continue play under Dugan's ruling."

The Abegweits and Dugan and the Mohawks and Foley took the field in Charlottetown two days later for what would be the series' most closely contested game. Leading 4-2 after eight innings, the Mohawks scored seven runs in the ninth. It ended all doubt, but not all of the drama.

During that inning, with men on base, Roy Boles poked the ball down the first base line. "That damn ball he hit kept rolling fair ... foul ... fair ... foul ... fair ... foul," recalls Orville Mitchell. "Christ, there was no place for it to go because the base line was hollowed out and the ball kept going back and forth."

Foley dashed out in front of the plate and made his call: "Fair!"

Abbie supporters, many of them emboldened with liquid courage, raged onto the field.

"These drunks were headin' right up towards the umpire," says Mitchell. "We all grabbed a bat. There were no policemen, and there must have been a thousand people there. They started going for Tush Foley, and Tush didn't back down from anybody. He was pretty good with his hands. He started walkin' right up towards them with his mask in his hand and his breast protector stickin' out."

The mob rushed towards Foley, who swaggered towards the mob. The gap closed to less than 30 feet.

"Get the hell back where you belong!" Foley barked, pointing up at the bleachers.

The mob continued in. Twenty feet. With every stride, Foley's threats grew sharper, the invectives more vile. Fifteen feet.

The entire St. Stephen team fell in behind their umpire. As the phalanxes came nose to nose, Foley pointed at Charlottetown catcher Shonna Francis, who was standing nearby.

"Ask him!" Foley shouted.

The intruders quieted and glared at Francis. The catcher paused, carefully eyeing the throng.

"It was fair," he said finally, shyly.

Silence.

Then, in the middle of the infield, the crowd turned on itself. "You lyin' son of a whore," one lout shouted to another. One swung a roundhouse right. Soon several fights broke out as Mohawk players stood with mouths agape and bats lowered. Foley watched for a moment, then snorted and turned away.

"Had Francis called it a foul ball," conjectured the *Courier*, "the matter would have become really serious; and having been told how hockey players have been beaten up on the Island, the Mohawks to a man tell how relieved they were when the tension was over."

The Mohawks returned home to a hero's welcome even grander than the celebration that followed the New Brunswick championship.

Tush Foley returned home with his stipend—$25, plus expenses.

HAT PINS, HORTONS
AND A HIDDEN BALL

"They were upset, but I don't think they knew
what happened themselves."
—George Purcell—

NINETEEN THIRTY-TWO was the last year St. Stephen considered the Depression a distant malady, and a political agitator named Hitler an insignificant enigma. Yet simplicity lingered in 1932—the year pussywillows bloomed in January.

St. Stephen was still the community where a man grew corn with six ears and a potato plant with 32 spuds, where an Ontario author named Margaret Laurence came to talk about books, where the Ganong Bros. chocolate factory became the first company on earth to sell candy in valentine heart boxes, and where a brother and sister swayed for 144-1/2 hours to win the Bella Vista Pavilion dance marathon, in nearby Bog Brook.

Here was a town where a gentleman named Ol' Steve appointed himself a one-man St. Croix Valley street cleaning department, sweeping, raking and stabbing spare bits of refuse from daylight until dark. With his broom, shovel and wheelbarrow, Ol' Steve patrolled. From time to time he would borrow a lawn mower, push it a half-mile into town, cut the grass around his favorite beer parlor, then push it home. All Ol' Steve wanted was a thank-you. And that's all he got.

It was the town where custodians of morality fought Satan and his evil drink, and awarded All Abstainers cards from the Women's Christian Temperance Union. "The powers of darkness challenge the existence of the Christian undertaking," the Reverend Percy Fitzpatrick would thunder. "We are not dealing with something harmless, but with a pernicious poison and habit-forming narcotic, a menace to our most cherished institutions...."

One of those institutions, although not necessarily cherished, was the town's weekly newspaper, the *Saint Croix Courier*.

Founded in 1865 by a 30-year-old English teacher, the *Courier* of the 1930s was owned and published by Stan Granville, a Saint John sea captain's son who shaped the newspaper in his own image: stern, neat, proper, predictable, respectable, conservative and Conservative. "He was as tight as the bark on the trees," says St. Stephen pitcher Roy Boles.

A staunch Baptist, Granville was over six feet tall and handsome, with the frosty bearing of an English aristocrat. A pair of pince-nez that balanced at the end of his nose added a scholarly dimension, and few dressed more nattily in all of the valley. He was seldom seen without a tie, even when he fished or hunted. His only flirtation with the traditional newsman's slovenliness was the cigarette that always protruded from the side of his mouth, ashes falling on his tie. He rarely drank.

Granville did not own a car until 1936 and, until then, walked a mile to the office and another mile back home. Usually, his work week lasted seven days and several nights. One of his few recreational outlets was his camp, located in a densely wooded area several miles out of town. Contrary to his appearance and to his profession, Stan Granville was astonishingly strong, which he demonstrated periodically by lifting large rolls of newsprint by himself, a job that ordinarily took two men.

The *Courier*'s staff numbered approximately a dozen and included three linotype operators, a couple of typesetters, a galley person or two, an editor and a reporter. Also included was a trio of pressmen who, on their hot-metal flatbed, printed other jobs—Ganong's candy wrappers, for example—in addition to the *Courier*. Granville treated the staff well enough by the day's standards, especially during hard times. "During the dry spells when there wasn't much work, he kept his employees, and they weren't doing a damn thing to earn the money," says Phil Rouse, a pressman with the *Courier* for more than 49 years.

Still, Granville maintained a distance from his employees. Fraternizing was as foreign to his managerial style as smiling was to his personality, and he required from his staff a discipline like his own. He was equally demanding with his two children. "We toed the line," says son Dick Granville, who inherited the paper from his father.

Nevertheless, Stan Granville was a community asset. He knew the

St. Croix Valley area about as well as anyone did, and he cared for its inhabitants. When it became obvious that the area could no longer do without a hospital, it was Stan Granville who spearheaded the successful drive to get one built.

That the *Saint Croix Courier* so completely bore the personal stamp of its owner was a mixed blessing. Granville was a friend of A. D. Ganong, the candy maker who had run successfully in the 1930 federal election. It was a victory partially attributable to the *Courier*'s unabashedly partisan coverage. Ganong's speeches were "clever," the nominating convention was "enthusiastic" and his life had "variety and scope." Judging by the *Courier*'s coverage, his Liberal opponent had but one characteristic— invisibility.

Despite this glaring partiality, the newspaper never officially declared itself Conservative, and the *Courier*'s 16 pages every Thursday morning offered diligent and regionally unsurpassed community journalism. A solid balance of business news, crime reporting, town coverage and sports stories largely avoided the ramblings and errors of the *Courier*'s contemporaries. From the county's outer regions came social notes on marriages, vacations, anniversaries and graduations written by local men and women eager for a byline and who were reliable enough to meet weekly deadlines.

Although fond of the St. Stephen ball team, Granville took no part in its founding or operation. He supported it through copious coverage of the local boys who could do no wrong. Well, almost no wrong. Orville Mitchell remembers when Granville criticized the team around 1934 for making mechanical errors. "He came out and really gave us quite a goin' over," Mitchell says. "[So at the next citizen's committee meeting] I had the paper and I took him to task over it. I said, 'Look, we are all amateurs. Most of us are married and got families and got jobs to do. We are never in tip-top shape. We are out there tired. Maybe some of us were up all night with a child, and you have the gall to sit on your big, fat ass in that office and write such a bunch of tripe like that for the people to read.' We wanted a retraction and didn't get it. But there was no more derogatory stories like that. He knew he had overstepped his bounds."

◆　◆　◆　◆

A men's service club, the Kiwanis Club of St. Stephen, now two years old, left its mark on the home town by assuming sponsorship of the senior baseball team from the Mohawk club. The latter organization was especially anxious to yield stewardship of its most time-consuming activity since Ganong Bros. president A. D. Ganong had reminded his son, Whidden, that he was in the candy business, not the baseball business, and to conduct himself accordingly. With the loss of Ganong, a driving force, and of other key organizers, the Mohawk club eventually abandoned even its bingo and card games. The club disappears from documents dating past 1932.

The Kiwanis changed the team's name from Mohawks to Kiwanis, bought new equipment and fitted players for new uniforms. The threadbare "M" sweatshirts were replaced by neat, grey, pin-striped livery with KIWANIS across the breast. If the team was going to play like the New York Yankees, reasoned the new management, the players may as well look like the Yankees.

In addition, the service club set up a baseball committee to raise funds through raffles and dances. The funds would allow for increased travel and improved drainage on the ball diamond. The president of the St. Stephen Kiwanis was the Reverend J. T. Ibbott, a handsome Anglican minister of about 40 who had recently arrived from St. Paul's Church in Halifax. He had been born in Britain, raised in Hamilton, Ontario, educated at Wycliffe College in Toronto and had served with the Royal Flying Corps during the First World War. He loved badminton more than baseball, but baseball was St. Stephen's game so Ibbott became an avid fan. The clergyman was also a solid money man who applied an accountant's definition of viability to the ball club.

The most important change Ibbott and the new management made was to withdraw the team from the York-Charlotte-Carleton Baseball League. By becoming one of the first Maritime teams to do so, St. Stephen could schedule most of its 25 or so games at home, save on travel costs and gear up for the more prestigious and more lucrative playoffs. For the rest of the decade the team would prepare for the playoffs by playing a full summer of exhibition games against local intermediate and senior teams from Fredericton and Saint John, and touring, or "barnstorming," American teams. One of the first and one of the most bizarre of the barnstorming teams was the New York Bloomer Girls.

The presence of women on Maritime baseball diamonds, although still uncommon, was not new.

In 1891, a touring American women's team had beaten several men's teams in Nova Scotia amid both support for female partici- pation and fears that women were physically and emotionally ill- suited for this activity. The Chicago Ladies encountered such opposition from a New Glasgow clergyman and from a Truro citizens' group, while the New Glasgow *Eastern Chronicle* called them "nothing better than a lot of hoodlums from a crowded city" and "frauds of the first order." However, warmer receptions awaited in Amherst, Moncton and Halifax, where a crowd of 3,000 came to the Wanderers Grounds to watch the Chicago Ladies beat a men's team 18-15.

By 1932, however, an appearance of the New York Bloomer Girls caused no such stir. Indeed, several unaffiliated teams were calling themselves Bloomer Girls in the 1930s. These teams were based in Kansas City, Boston, New York and Texas. Several teams had both men and women on their rosters, including future major league star pitchers "Smokey Joe" Wood and Hall of Famer Rogers Hornsby. The Texas Bloomer Girls carried a "one-armed boy who plays center field." Despite the number of Bloomer Girls teams, no formal league was established, and they did not play each other.

One of the best of the Bloomer Girls cluster faced the Kiwanis in August 1932. Alias the New York College Girls Baseball Club, the New York Bloomer Girls were a disparate troupe of women who played baseball in the summer and basketball in the winter, and who claimed to be college graduates—a contention neither challenged nor proven by a sexist, servile press. "While no player is hired for beauty alone," said the *Telegraph-Journal*, "there are several girls who would get serious consideration in a beauty show."

The New York Bloomer Girls hustled the eastern United States during the 1920s and turned curiosity into currency throughout the Maritimes in the next decade. In 1929, they played 166 games, 133 of them on the road and 33 in the New York City area. By contrast, major league teams played only 154 games, half of them at home. The Bloomer Girls boasted several highly skilled athletes, including shortstop Peggy O'Neill, outfielder Dot Warren, who could throw strikes from deep centre, and pitcher Harriett Smith, who stood close to six feet tall and owned butcher's forearms. Oddest of the lot was slightly built Betty Burch, a catcher who wore a mask but eschewed shin guards and chest protector, although she posed for photographs wearing the latter. Burch explained that the equipment hindered her throws to second base.

Clever publicity preceded the Bloomer Girls-Kiwanis encounter in 1932. "My mates and myself feel sure we will receive cordial treatment from your fans and your players," captain O'Neill wrote to Kiwanis management. "Still we will feel matters will be more even if one of our own sex will call them as she sees them." The *Courier* speculated about who would fill that role, and the question increased interest in a game destined to be more novelty than contest. Eventually, local track star Dorothy Norwood, known in the 1920s as the Maritimes' best female athlete, volunteered to be umpire.

Nevertheless, the management of the defending Maritime senior baseball champions did not take the whole affair very seriously. Team mascot Billy Moffatt started in the outfield. Catcher Muddy McLain and centre fielder Gordon Coffey each pitched. Several players, however, could not suppress their competitive impulse. "They were advertised as champions of the United States," recalls Roy Boles, "and I thought, 'Well, I'm going to have to pitch and I don't want them hitting me all over the field,' so I was throwing curve balls. I thought they could hit, but they couldn't. The girl on the second base was a left-hand batter, and I threw a curve ball to her and it broke in on her and it hit her in the chest. Right in the breasts! I thought, 'Oh Jesus!' She dropped on the ground and held on to her chest. I'm there on the mound, 'What have I done? I've hit a girl!'"

The Bloomer Girl was not badly hurt, but Boles threw no more curves during the peculiar exhibition that resuscitated an ailing Kiwanis team treasury and attracted 500 paying spectators, many of them women.

The Kiwanis won 6-3.

The team began a protracted playoff schedule that season by sweeping Fredericton in two straight games, then winning the first game of a best-of-three semi-final against Grand Falls. Game two was played before 1,500 fans in Grand Falls—an Irish farming town of about 2,000 in northwestern New Brunswick—on a dusty diamond near an 80-foot waterfall.

"The infield was tolerable and it did have a pitcher's mound, but in the outfield a combination of long grass and hidden gopher holes made the pursuit of a long fly ball a steeplechase, and a bushy growth of clover back of third base permitted several low-average hitters their only triples and home runs of their lives," New Brunswick journalist David Folster wrote in the *Atlantic Advocate* of his home town's facility.

"The truly distinguishing feature, however, was in right-field and right-centre. There, a town roadway composed of gravel hardened to a concrete texture cut smack across, accompanied thirty feet above by electric and telephone lines. This circumstance turned up endless possibilities, not the least being the electrocution of an outfielder," Folster wrote.

This outlandish setting tested a man's creativity. "One of their players hit an infield pop up," says first baseman Orville Mitchell. "I was just standing there waiting and the ball hit one of the wires and landed 20 feet in front of me. That made the bases full, and there was only one out. So I walked over to [St. Stephen pitcher] Jack Hill and said, 'Don't get back on the mound,' and I hid the ball in my glove. Then I went back and tagged the guy off second base. That's actually the first time I ever tried the hidden ball trick."

The Kiwanis won the game in Grand Falls 12-5 to sweep the series and advance to the New Brunswick finals against the Saint John Martellos. The Martellos, with aging Charlie Gorman a lesser force than he had been in 1931, were again Saint John city champions, and they sought to avenge their abrupt elimination by St. Stephen the year before. A thousand fans watched game one of the finals in St. Stephen as Jack Hill, an addition to the team from nearby Black's Harbour, faced an unflappable farmer named "Iron Man" Ira Hannah.

The Iron Man, who was sometimes late for games because he had to milk his cows, had a particular rhythm to his pitching—slow, deliberate, annoying. "He'd throw the ball, then walk half way up to the catcher, get the ball, then walk back all the way around the mound. Every time. It took a little time," recalls Saint John pitcher Lefty Brownell.

Brownell recalls that when Hannah's arm used to bother him, he would roll up his sleeve, take out a bottle of something and massage in some of the substance. One time Brownell suffered a muscle twitch while pitching and Hannah told Brownell to try some of his cure. "So I put a little on—I was sweating at the time. Then, when I pitched, I didn't know if I had a sore arm or any kind of arm at all.

I didn't feel a thing. He gave me horse liniment."

Hannah lasted just two innings in losing game one, 6-5. Two days later, at Saint John's North End Improvement League diamond, he tied the series with a six-hit 4-3 victory. The deciding game of the series was a showcase for the magnificent Roy Boles. He beat Hannah 5-2, holding the Martellos to six hits, while going four-for-five at the plate and scoring twice. It was St. Stephen's second straight New Brunswick championship.

The Kiwanis' next challenge came from the improved Charlottetown Abegweits. Baseball popularity on Prince Edward Island had slipped in the early 1930s, and this team with new faces and new ambitions hoped to rekindle interest. The Abbies had demolished Summerside 9-0 and 20-3 to win the Island title, but the Kiwanis were a vastly more potent foe, and they waltzed past Charlottetown into the Maritime final with 8-1 and 6-2 wins, the latter a 12-inning victory by Boles.

Meanwhile in Nova Scotia, a team with pedigree charged through that province's playdowns confident that they, the Yarmouth Gateways, were the best ballplayers in the Maritimes, perhaps in all of amateur Canada.

◆   ◆   ◆   ◆

An historic shipbuilding centre and a refuge during the American Revolution, in the 1930s Yarmouth was an easy blend of light industry, small business and moneyed Americans. Its location on the tip of Nova Scotia's South Shore earned it the moniker Gateway to the Maritimes and ensured it a slightly cosmopolitan atmosphere. Yarmouth's 7,000 inhabitants loved their ocean and their sports—especially baseball.

Organized baseball had begun in Yarmouth in 1909 with the Resolutes, who that year beat Middleton for the Nova Scotia championship and beat the Saint John Roses for the Maritime crown. The next year, a wealthy New Englander formed a second team, St. Ambrose, and in the mid-1920s a semi-professional league began. It survived only two seasons but spawned at least one memorable talent, outfielder Jersey Joe Stripp. The native of Harrison, New Jersey, played 1,146 games for four National League teams, ending his career with 24 home runs and a .294 batting average.

The Gateways senior team was organized in 1928 by the Yarmouth

Amateur Athletic Association, which, like the Kiwanis' management, booked a summer exhibition schedule featuring several barnstorming teams. Four years later the Gateways were a successful amalgam of veteran and novice that had lost just once in 27 games entering the provincial finals. This stunning record was achieved without their regular right fielder, Edgar (Lightning) Amirault, who in the summer of '32 was running more than base paths.

◆ ◆ ◆ ◆

After Prohibition was declared in the United States in 1920, the young men of Yarmouth, feeling that there is a no more sorrowful image than a thirsty Yankee with money, summoned their innate seafaring skills and headed off to do the right thing. "I had to do something," says Amirault. "I couldn't stay on shore and live on love."

Rumrunning was in Amirault's blood. He practised it in the company of virtuosos after learning it from his father, a wily, veteran runner whose lone blemish was an eight-month stint in a Canton, New Jersey, jail. Police patrols were a nuisance for Maritime rumrunners, but the rate of capture was astonishingly low. Many authorities were bribed into blindness, but runners were sage seamen with a derring-do since romanticized in local lore. "I called it a game of the hare and the hound," says Lightning Amirault. "In the afternoon, they'd get close, and we'd try to get away from them at night. We'd put on a smoke screen and pretty soon we'd be gone."

Aboard a 120-foot vessel named *Accuracy*, Amirault would be gone for three months at a stretch, living, laughing and sweating with a dozen men of disparate backgrounds. "We'd go down St.-Pierre and load up 4,200 cases and go off to New York or Block Island [in Rhode Island] to get rid of them. Sometimes, you'd go down to Bermuda and make a double-header, we'd call it. We'd get $50 extra."

Amirault says the rumrunners did little drinking on the ships, waiting until they reached St.-Pierre, where the stores sold it to exporters. "They had these barrels of wine, and they'd say, 'Go ahead, boys, try some.' By the time you'd get to the end of them barrels—five or six of 'em, and you'd drink out of each one—you'd be feelin' pretty good," Amirault says.

"The first time I ever got to feeling good was off the coast of New

York, Christmas Day, 1930. The captain comes down at noon and says, 'Boys, we can't go ashore for Christmas dinner, but we can have a drink, anyway.' He had two bottles of champagne and he opened them both."

One bright day in 1932, about 150 miles off the coast of Halifax, a savage storm crashed down from nowhere and ripped the *Accuracy*'s sails, sending the crew scurrying. For two days gale-force winds pounded the vessel and the crew begrudgingly tossed overboard 150 cases of Jamaica rum to help stay afloat. By the second day, the skipper felt that all was lost, and he quietly prepared to meet his maker. "If that storm would have happened at night," says Amirault, "we'd have lost it for sure."

He was at sea the entire baseball season of 1932, returning mysteriously to the line-up for the Maritime final against the Kiwanis. The press announced his return but did not explain his absence.

Amirault and half a dozen other players formed the core of a supreme amateur baseball team in Yarmouth, but two men in particular were cardinal figures throughout the decade. One was coach Ernie Grimshaw, a tough-minded mentor and, in 1932, the Gateways' second baseman. The other was Halley Horton, a baby-faced shortstop exalted throughout the region for his skills and sportsmanship, and a young man distracted by love. Until pretty Harriet McRoy returned from school in Cleveland, Ohio, Horton would dash regularly to the nearest telegraph office and send staccato dispatches—dominated by game scores—across the 49th parallel. In 1932, the messages were usually sweet.

The Gateways had hammered Liverpool and Halifax in the first two playoff rounds. The Halifax triumph, in particular, had ignited spontaneous celebrations throughout Yarmouth. The new champions were feted at banquets, and the mayor declared half-holidays on game days for all furture games that year. Townspeople, some barely living from meal to meal, donated money to fund the team's travel. A Gateways official had even invented a snappy little jig in honor of the provincial final. And in front of the Majestic Theatre on Main Street, approximately 500 fans cheered and held up traffic for half an hour as the team boarded a chartered bus that was bedecked in Gateway orange and black and sporting the banner, The Gateway Champions En Route To Reserve.

◆ ◆ ◆ ◆

The Reserve Miner Boys were idols in the coal mining town of 2,500 about five miles from Glace Bay, Cape Breton. Baseball on Cape Breton dated back to the turn of the century, with teams of imported players wearing the uniform—some featuring high sneakers and bow ties—of Sydney, Sydney Mines, Reserve Mines and Glace Bay. Still, the first Cape Breton team ever to reach the Nova Scotia senior finals was the Reserve Miner Boys in 1932.

The Miner Boys' diamond was not enclosed, so Reserve management switched the games to Glace Bay's South Street grounds—a facility that hugged the Atlantic shore and offered little protection from chilling autumn sea breezes. Nevertheless, for game one of the provincial final a huge crowd gathered, occasionally encroaching on the field and constantly straining at ropes along the foul lines.

One interested spectator was a massive Scot named Sandy who plunked himself directly behind the visiting team's bench and berated the Gateways incessantly for two games. "Bye da lard Jaysus, youse gonna git da shit put ta ya, t'day, byes," he said again and again. "We were glad when a Mountie came over and stood behind our bench," says Halley Horton. "Once, he looked up and said, 'By da lard Jaysus, any dozen of ya come and git me.' He wasn't going to be pushed around, and he was having a good time, too. All he had on was this T-shirt, and it was really cold. The dust was blowin' on that skin diamond and his eyes were full of dirt, and the dirt was all running down his face. And he rode us and he rode us, but nobody dared say a word back. When we went back the next day for the second game he was right there in the same condition. Same shirt on. Same mud running down his cheeks. And he kept riding us."

Despite the heckling, Yarmouth won the first game 5-0. Reserve tied the series with a 9-4 win in game two, as a frigid gale swept clouds of dust from home plate to centre field, compelling the Gateways to don heavy sweater coats.

After the game Halley Horton optimistically telegraphed to his love, Harriet: "THIS IS THE BEST WE COULD DO TODAY.... YOU CAN, HOWEVER, FIGURE US AS NS CHAMPS ANYWAY. SEE YOU LATER.—HALLEY"

Back in Yarmouth, the Gateways beat the Miner Boys twice to win the series, despite a cold northwest wind that swayed pitchers as they stood on the mound. More than 2,500 fans watched in overcoats. Again, Yarmouthians celebrated. In the hotels, on the wharves and along Main Street, they whooped it up for two days. Fire trucks with the two teams atop and scores of cars led a merry procession of fans bearing torches and Roman candles. Rockets fired, car horns blared. And Halley Horton ran to the telegraph office to share the joy with Cleveland, Ohio: "HAIL THE CHAMPS, KID. WE WON BOTH GAMES HERE—HALLEY"

◆ ◆ ◆ ◆

The Yarmouth-St. Stephen Maritime final was the first clash of the decade's two dominant teams. Moreover, the series linked the names of the Gateways' Doug Horton (Halley's older brother) and of the Kiwanis' Orville Mitchell—forever bonded by one game, one play, one moment.

Exaggeration dogged Doug Horton, a powerful man with a face dominated by a Roman nose. At age 25 and standing six-foot-two, he was often thought to be older and taller. His home runs were also exaggerated, although several of them required no embellishment. And his ego? Horton never cared much that his little brother, Halley, was Nova Scotia's most popular baseball player. (In the middle of the decade Halley would top a readers' poll in a Halifax newspaper and would be declared Nova Scotia's Most Popular Ball Player.)

Doug Horton had attained this humility the hard way, as a cocky former high school star playing his first senior level game. "That first game I had five balls hit to me, and I made five errors," Horton remembers. "The sixth man hit a ball to me, and I went in front of [the] shortstop and threw a perfect ball to first base, and the first baseman just put his glove out and let the ball go by. Never even tried to stop it. I was so mad I just cried right there on the field. And there was quite a crowd in the stands. After it was over I went down in the clubhouse and the coach looked at me and said, 'You're not so hard, are ya?'"

Nor was life easy off the field. Married with children, Doug Horton had only spotty employment during the decade. He worked at odd jobs, shoveled snow, filled in at the post office and received just enough credit to get by. In 1936, he started a garbage business that, in the beginning, brought in an average of just 45 cents a week. "There was lots of times I didn't know if the family was going to have something on their plates for dinner or not. Thankfully, they always had something to eat."

The mercurial economics of the 1930s were gentler on St.

Stephen's Orville Mitchell. He found work with a lumber company and a Calais shoe factory before joining Canadian Customs, eventually becoming collector and supervising a staff of 42.

A semi-professional in the St. Croix Baseball League in the 1920s, Mitchell's hawk-like facial features and his deep rich voice gave him a commanding presence. His directions seemed more palatable, his jokes funnier, his observations wiser. Often he played first or second base and coached at the same time.

But Mitchell did not merely play baseball, he dissected it— constantly cultivating an appreciation for nuances and seeking openings to exploit little-known legalities. He viewed the sport from a higher intellectual plateau and crawled inside it. Sometimes at night he lay awake for hours and replayed a game, eyes boring a hole in the ceiling, anguishing over missed opportunities and contemplating alternative strategies. "Mitchell knows the game from A to Z," said the *Saint Croix Courier* in a brief profile, "and if the occasional error is chalked up against him it is a slip of the hand, not of the head."

"You ran a team like a poker game," says Mitchell. "You had to play the percentages. You ran your team on the analysis of each player, what he was capable of doing the best. You gave him a sign when he went to the plate. Bunt? Hit and run? Wait out the pitch? You'd have to read the pitcher first, look at his flaws, watch his motion, how he holds the ball. You can tell if it's a curve or a fast ball. And you can steal the signs from the catcher during the game."

Not every move was calculated, however.

"I was playin' first base one time and at a certain time of year when the sun would be setting, it would be in line with the batter and the pitcher. The catcher wouldn't dare throw the ball down because I couldn't see it. Somebody hit a pop fly, and of course I was looking and I was running. I had my hand up and I hit the bag with my toe and fell down. You could hear the groans from the crowd. But I didn't take my eye off the ball, and I was still lying on the ground goin' for it. And I put my glove up and the ball dropped in it. There was oohs and ahs. I said, 'Anybody could have caught the ball standing up. I thought I'd give you something a little spectacular.'"

◆ ◆ ◆ ◆

Game one of the 1932 Maritime finals in St. Stephen produced a 5-3 St. Stephen win and a major altercation between Yarmouth's

Halley Horton and Kiwanis umpire Tush Foley. In the fourth inning, with men on first and second, Horton smashed a pitch over the head of left fielder Ike Vanstone. Horton sprinted home to tie the game, only to learn that Foley claimed Horton had not tagged third base. Horton was out and his critical run disallowed. A nearly identical play had happened the previous week in the Nova Scotia final against Reserve, and now the twice-burned Horton threw his hands skyward in disbelief.

Horton still insists the call was wrong, perhaps deliberately so. He remembers third base coach Ernie Grimshaw yelling, "Touch that bag! You've got plenty of time!"

So Horton touched that bag "solid."

Still, he was called out. "We were tipped off about Foley. There was this ... Saint John fellow called one of our guys to tell him that Foley was a cutie. And he was cute enough that he only called the critical plays."

After Roy Boles' four-hitter in game one, Howdy Clark and his Nothin' Ball stopped the Gateways 5-1 in game two. Clark was at his best, and just two days after his wife had given birth to a baby boy.

Immediately following the game the Gateways drove to Saint John, then caught the Digby ferry home. It was a pensive trip. The town of Yarmouth had sent them off with grand expectations, and the press had picked them to win. Now this talented team with only two losses prior to this series needed to sweep three straight games from a team with no obvious weakness.

Perhaps to mask this conundrum, Gateways management turned its wrath on Foley and lobbied for another umpire in game three. "Public sentiment was strongly against the appearance of the New Brunswick umpire on the Yarmouth field," stated the *Halifax Herald*. "Demands were insistent for a neutral umpire and it is quite possible that fans may force the issue." Yarmouth management considered filing a protest if St. Stephen insisted on Foley, but soon the team abandoned the idea. So in game three it was Foley, but in game three it was irrelevant.

The Gateways came out strongly and banished Kiwanis ace Boles in the first inning. "There was a smile on Roy Boles' face as he stepped to the mound," wrote Ace Foley in the *Halifax Chronicle*, "perhaps a smile of disdain. Hadn't he halted those Gateway boys with a few scattered hits last week? That smile soon faded." Murray

Veno singled to centre. Nate Bain bunted safely. Halley Horton singled. Pete White walked. Red Goudey singled through second. Doug Horton cracked a fastball over the left field fence and onto the street. The final score was 10-1.

The decisive win partially avenged the laceration of community pride felt earlier in the week. So that night in the middle of the Great Depression, Yarmouth, Nova Scotia, danced. The town laughed and sang and marched and chanted, "Three straight, three straight!" The local weekly newspaper, the *Yarmouth Herald*, ran front-page prognostications of doom for the Kiwanis, while in the *Halifax Chronicle* Foley wrote that the Gateways "are determined there won't be another loss. They must win. And, believe me, I think they will."

Gateways coach Grimshaw thought so, too, and took his certainty to the streets, taunting Kiwanis players as they walked to their hotel after the game. "I didn't know whether he was drinkin' or what," says Roy Boles. "We were comin' down the street, me and Harry [Boles] and one other player. And him and another guy was behind us—about 20 feet—and they took at us, what they were goin' to do to us tomorrow and all that stuff. He was threatening us, callin' us all kinds of names and everything. That guy always wanted to fight."

With the Kiwanis' mystique evaporated and the Gateways again confident, more than 1,500 people gathered at the Yarmouth diamond the next afternoon for game four. The St. Stephen players suddenly realized that, for the first time in two years, they confronted a team of peers, and even with Clark pitching at his peak, they had to exploit every advantage and avoid key errors.

The big hit of game four came in the seventh inning. Returning from an injury a few innings before, St. Stephen catcher Muddy McLain, stitches around his eye, slashed a Cliffie Surrette pitch off the centre-field fence. That knocked the pitcher out of the game and helped the Kiwanis jump in front 4-0. Yarmouth players planted the seeds of a comeback in their half of the seventh but scored just once. St. Stephen, on the other hand, scored three more in the top of the ninth to take a 7-1 lead.

The Gateways fought on. In the bottom of the ninth, Halley Horton singled, went to second, then scored on an infield out. Seven-two. Next, Doug Horton singled past shortstop, reaching second on an outfield error. The stage was now set for one of the decade's most discussed plays.

It began with a slow survey of the situation by Orville Mitchell, the Kiwanis second baseman. "We were hangin' on, and I felt in my bones that the next fella up was gonna get a hit," he says.

Mitchell took the belated throw from the outfield—where Horton's hit had rolled—then strolled in to Clark, the ball in his glove. Standing alongside his pitcher, Mitchell bluffed placing the ball in Clark's glove and, instead, flicked it back into his own glove. Clark casually turned his back to Horton, who began inching off the bag. Mitchell jogged back to his position.

Surreptitiously watching Horton's movements, the Kiwanis' veteran infielder settled a couple of yards on the other side of the base.

Mitchell crouched down, then feigned a move towards Horton.

The runner stepped briskly back to the base.

Mitchell crouched down again.

It was Horton's move.

"I think the umpire [Jimmy Amiro of Yarmouth] might have got a glimpse of the ball in my glove," says Mitchell. "Anyway, the next time I let [Horton] go as far as I figured I could beat him to the bag. He was about six feet off, and I was about six feet off. But I got the jump on him, and of course I made a dive for the last part of it, and I caught him off second. He was tryin' to get back. But I had him dead-to-rights."

Mitchell tagged Horton. The hidden-ball trick had worked perfectly.

Says Doug Horton: "It's just wide-awake baseball. Until the pitcher had the ball in his hands I had no business taking my foot off the base. If I had been concentrating, I'd have stayed on the base. You're bound to be embarrassed—the last out of the ball game and you're playin' for the Maritime title. I tried to knock the ball out of his glove, but I couldn't ... I could have knocked his bloody head off, to tell you the truth."

After being tagged out, Horton stood on the base and gazed straight ahead. Teammates moaned but said nothing to the first baseman, to whom they had turned frequently for towering, decisive hits at crucial junctures. Now, in his moment of ignominy, Doug Horton mourned alone.

The jubilant Kiwanis were not accorded such privacy. Gateway supporters roared onto the field in pursuit of any pin-striped New Brunswicker they could nab. Seeing the charge, Mitchell scooped up the ball and, with his mates close behind, dashed for the St. Stephen cars parked behind the grandstand.

"They were hittin' us and throwin' stuff and everything," says outfielder George Purcell. "They were throwin' anything they could get their hands on. Rocks, anything. And kickin' and kickin' at you. They were upset, but I don't think they knew what happened themselves."

"They were callin' us cheaters and crooks," remembers Mitchell. "And the women in those days had hat pins to keep their hats on their head. They chased us right into the cars. They were jabbin' some of the players in the backsides as we crawled into the cars. And once we got into the cars we pulled the curtains and put the windows up. We got out of that park some quick."

A prime target of hat pins, rocks, insults and threats was Tush Foley, although the final call had been made by Jimmy Amiro, Yarmouth's umpiring nominee. Miraculously, Foley was unharmed.

"We drove right up to the Grand Hotel and ran right up to our rooms," says Mitchell. "That night, we just entertained among ourselves. Some of the boys went out and had a few beers, but we played poker till four or five in the morning. And maybe we drank a little beer. But we all pretty well stuck to the hotel because we didn't want to get out and get involved in the street with anybody."

Actually, there was little to fear. Yarmouth's Main Street in the aftermath was as barren and listless as the town's spirit. The silent night was cut only by a ballplayer's lament that clicked to Cleveland, Ohio: "ST. STEPHEN WINS CHAMPIONSHIP. WE JUST COULDN'T MAKE IT.—HALLEY."

REIGN, REIGN, GO AWAY

"If it wasn't for you, you son of a bitch, we would have won."
—A Springhill spectator—

AS THE HOLLOW-EYED HUNGRY traversed the nation in search of hope, Canada's 123rd relief camp opened on the Old Back Road outside of Fredericton, about 70 miles north of St. Stephen. Operated by the military, the camps offered an alternative to the filthy railway jungles and, according to the federal government, delivered men from "conditions of misery in the cities and [gave] them a reasonable standard of living and comfort." At the Depression's bottom, more than 200 camps existed in Canada, most of them housing 100 to 200 men.

On the Old Back Road, former laborers, factory workers, fishermen and farmers slogged with pick and shovel for 40 hours a week to build dams, roads, army huts and a forestry experimental station. The camp provided shelter, food, razor, toothbrush, medical treatment, emergency dental treatment, hospitalization and a limited ration of tobacco and cigarettes. The wage was 20 cents a day.

"Single, unemployed men on relief may at first glance think the cash remuneration is inadequate," reasoned the commander of Military District No. 7 in Saint John. "The proposal is worth more careful investigation as it is considered that the situation of the men so engaged compares favorably with that of the single men who are employed for short periods, at the present low rate of wages, and have in the intervals to provide themselves with board and lodgings. After these men have paid their board bill, bought their clothes, boots and rubbers, tobacco or cigarettes, paid their laundry, doctor, dentist and hospital bills, would they over a period have $5.00 or $6.00 in cash left over each month? A very careful man in one of these camps might have a moderate bank account at the end of the year."

The price, of course, was a man's dignity. The work was meaningless and unproductive, and it provided no reasonable outlet for the energies of males in the prime of their lives. The camps spent nothing on recreation. Magazines were rare. Although free to desert this empty existence, most men had no place else to go. So they stayed at the Old Back Road and at scores of similar shelters across the country.

Few men from St. Stephen toiled on the Old Back Road. To the contrary, the town was targeted by Americans and Canadians wandering workless whose feeble taps on back doors became the era's most poignant descant. The welcome was sometimes cool.

"The gentleman of leisure, who come to this part of the country in the summer months," editorialized the *Saint Croix Courier*, "constitute a nuisance, and to some degree a menace to the peace and security of the housewife from whom, in large part, they beg a comfortable living. It is to be questioned whether the tender-hearted women who so frequently assist these men think of the probable consequences of their generosity. While it is true that the plight of most of these tramps seems to invite sympathy and kindness, it is equally true that their condition is equally of their own making, for there is no necessity of the able-bodied hiking about the country making their living off others who are willing to work. When these men are fed generously in a community, that town quickly earns the name among the begging fraternity as an 'easy' place to work, and the first visitors return again and bring new ones with them. Visitors of their type are a nuisance to the town and in numbers they may become a pronounced menace, especially if intoxicants become available."

Despite the setback of two major fires in 1933, St. Stephen barely felt the economic downturn. Summers Fertilizer Company, which employed 30 men and would hire 10 more during the next three years, reported good years in 1932 and 1933, as did Ganong Bros. The Canadian Cottons Ltd. mill in Milltown increased its weekly payroll by $2,500.

Granted, a substantial amount of this success was reaped from the sweat and exploitation of the workers. The mill, for example, sold coal to its employees, immediately removing the cost of the coal from their pay envelopes. The father of St. Stephen outfielder George Purcell was a loom fixer at the mill, and the despair on his father's face when he opened his weekly stipend haunts Purcell to this day. "I can still hear my father say, 'That's a pretty poor pay.' But we had to keep warm, and that soft coal—they used it in their boiler room—was the only means. You could buy hardwood, but you'd pay more money for that. Coal was cheaper. And they kept their wages small."

If wages were low, however, so was unemployment. It was a trade-off most local people could accept.

For its few poor, the Town of St. Stephen set aside about $80 from a weekly budget of $1,300. (The total paid in town relief in 1933 was $4,000.) A qualifying husband and wife received $3 a week, plus proportionate increases based on the number of dependents—if the man worked approximately 12 hours per week for the town. The families could then buy goods from a local merchant, who, in turn, recorded the items and amounts and passed the information back to town officials. As well, relief recipients could chop wood for the town and take home half of what they cut. Nevertheless, this charity lashed at a man's pride, and entire families experienced a wrenching sense of helplessness.

Perhaps no man in the St. Croix Valley received more charity, or seemed more worthy of it, than an old ballplayer named Eke Johnson. A congenial man in his 50s, Johnson had undertaken several worthy community efforts in his younger and more able years. By the 1930s, though, he was battling severe arthritis and had had a leg amputated. So frequent fund-raising events were held in his honor, and the Eke Johnson Benefit Game became part of the Kiwanis team schedule. Bingos and various social affairs were also held, including a benefit movie—ironically, *Hopalong Cassidy*—to help ease Johnson's lot.

After each event Johnson would send a letter off to the local newspaper. "There are some acts in this world that mere words of thanks cannot ever repay," he wrote. "I want you all to know that I am receiving this generous aid in the spirit of genuine gratitude. This may not be the proper time and manner to do this, but hang the odds! I want to thank all dear friends who called on me during my 10 weeks in the Chipman Hospital."

The good will towards Johnson was exceptional, however. Indeed, many St. Stephenites considered their stricken neighbors and countrymen to be slothful. When inmates of British Columbia relief camps embarked on their ill-fated On To Ottawa Trek and received thousands of dollars in food and clothing along the way, the *Courier* thundered that such communal largess was "a typical example of the kind of maudlin sympathy that is making it more and more difficult to retain respect for law and order." Besides, said the newspaper, it was likely a Communist publicity stunt.

Amid St. Stephen's relative affluence, baseball money was nevertheless scarce. The team cost between $2,000 and $3,000 each season to run. The Kiwanis Club of St. Stephen, which a year earlier had taken over operations from the Mohawk club, buckled under its sponsorship obligation and the time required to run the team. The *Courier* reported that the Kiwanis club was "not keen in taking over the team again unless assurances were forthcoming from a group of representative citizens that outside backing would be given.... As everyone knows, the team is absolutely embarrassed financially. We will not make any extraordinary appeal to harass the public for funds, although unsolicited contributions would be as welcome as manna from heaven."

Outfielder Gordon Coffey says that the Kiwanis used to guarantee opposing teams a certain amount of money per game. During the 1932 season, a number of games had been rained out, and the Kiwanis club lost a fair amount of money. Not surprisingly the service club wanted out of the baseball business. "They said they would pay for our registration if we would play under the Kiwanis name, so we did," Coffey recalls.

At the time the ball team's only university graduate, Coffey was appointed manager at the beginning of the 1933 season. But everyone, including Coffey, soon realized that the job required a more experienced hand. "I didn't have the know-how to contact outside teams," Coffey says. He eventually stepped aside and a citizens' committee was established to run the team. The committee included some familiar names: the Reverend J. T. Ibbott, Kiwanis president, and Bill Whitlock, co-founder of the Mohawk club. However, the key man to enlist was 36-year-old Len Webber.

In the 1930s Webber worked for Canadian Customs and was therefore well-connected on both sides of the border. Low-key and well-organized, the wounded veteran of the First World War tapped into this international network to book top American touring teams to play the Kiwanis. "He never approved of us playing the same old duds all the time," says Mitchell. "We learned because 90 percent of the time with these teams, we were playing above our heads."

Webber's ever-present pipe gave him a highbrow aura that helped compensate for his unimposing physical stature. "The first time I saw him," says Coffey, "I didn't think he was going to live very long. He was just a skeleton with the skin hauled over it."

Webber was recognized as one of the province's best sports executives. In 1935 he was elected president of the New Brunswick Amateur Baseball Association, introducing to that body a new order and meticulousness. His affiliation with the St. Stephen baseball team lasted until the end of the decade.

Part of his duties with the Kiwanis team was to oversee the fund-raising blitz conducted for a week or two each spring. High school girls recruited by teacher Gordon Coffey canvassed door-to-door from early morning until nine o'clock at night. Their pitch was, "Do your part to keep the name of this community up where it belongs, at the head of the list of sporting towns in the Maritimes!" Tag Day 1933 netted $93. "Highly gratifying," said the citizens' committee. A card party at St. Patrick's Hall raised bucks for bats and balls, while clam-chowder suppers helped, too. Game attendance increased as well, due in no small part to Kiwanis wins in their first six games.

In St. Stephen baseball was more than just popular. By 1933 it was becoming stylish.

Two important roster changes occurred that year. Cotton-mill employee Bill McIntosh substituted at second base for Orville Mitchell, who was ill much of the summer. A gifted fielder who cut the palm out of his glove to feel the ball better, McIntosh had once played professionally in Maine.

The second addition was taxi driver Charlie Godfrey, an outfielder converted to catcher whose physical conditioning was better suited to playing pool, which he preferred to baseball. "We would go out and run the bases, and when we were finished, Charlie would just be a lather of sweat," recalls a teammate. "Halfway through, the uniform would be soaking wet. As soon as we'd be done practising, Charlie would go have [a] shower and have a couple of milk shakes." Godfrey also favored a local hot dog stand where he would consume four or five of the house specials each day. He often instructed his pitchers to throw high balls because catching low ones was too much work. "I used to wonder how he'd get down on the low balls because of that paunch," says Gordon Coffey. Nevertheless, Godfrey was an excellent hitter, even though "he had to hit the ball a mile just to get to first base."

The pitching would again be handled by Roy Boles and Howdy Clark. A third hurler, an extremely handsome left-hander named Laurie Crompton, saved his best pitches for Maritime maidens who fell for his overtures in remarkable numbers.

Congenial coach Arthur Middlemiss returned, too, minus part of one finger—the result of an accident in the candy factory.

The Kiwanis combination was good enough during that 1933 season to make the team victorious in 80 percent of their games. They carried the momentum into the first rounds of the provincial playoffs, where they manhandled the team from Devon, a small community just outside Fredericton. The New Brunswick final matched the Kiwanis and St. Peter's, the survivors of the Saint John City League.

St. Peter's was led by a bespectacled and prematurely cantankerous 24-year-old mason named Cecil (Lefty) Brownell. One of the decade's best pitchers, Brownell was enjoying one of the decade's best years, and he sought to crown his glorious season with a provincial championship.

One September Saturday, 1,500 people endured a crisp wind and watched the Kiwanis detonate Brownell's dream, slashing him to all corners of the diamond for 15 hits. St. Stephen won that game 10-3, then the next day thumped another St. Peter's pitcher, 11-3. A few days later in Saint John, the Kiwanis again beat Brownell, 4-2, for their third consecutive provincial championship.

Some Kiwanis players say Brownell wept after the final loss. The intense southpaw disputes the tears. True or not, for St. Stephen it was the final of least resistance; for Brownell, it was devastation. For all, however, it turned out to be a wonderful opportunity. After the 1933 season, Kiwanis management would offer to secure Brownell a job in St. Stephen, and Brownell would come to the border—to lay bricks, play for the Kiwanis and complete the foundation of a baseball dynasty.

Meanwhile, in a neighboring province, another group of athletes was on a roll. Powered by a 22-year-old former Moncton CCs southpaw named Copie LeBlanc, the Springhill Fence Busters swept past Halifax to win the Nova Scotia senior championship.

The Maritime semi-final between Springhill and the Charlottetown Abegweits included unrelenting rains that caused postponement after postponement. (Before the first semi-final game, scheduled for Springhill, Fence Busters' coach Jim Conway and an Abegweit representative sloshed through town to inspect the field. "Where's the diamond?" asked the Islander, gazing upon a murky lake. "I'll be blowed!" said Conway. "It's gone!")

Surveyors would wade through the high water and drive stakes where the diamond was last seen. They had had plenty of practice: in the late summer and early autumn of 1933 the Springhill diamond had been submerged eight times.

"This is my third visit to Springhill in the last three weeks," complained Halifax columnist Ace Foley, "and on each occasion I have seen more rain here than I care to see for an entire summer. It doesn't seem possible that there is any left up above but there must be because it's still falling."

Eventually, the series opener was moved to Charlottetown, where the Fence Busters won 6-0. Back in Springhill before 400 shivering spectators—the smallest crowd of the season—they swept the series with a 14-0 thrashing, mercifully terminated after seven innings. Forbearance, it seemed, was ingrained in Springhill.

Springhill, Nova Scotia, was cursed with abundant coal deposits. In 1891, two years after the town was incorporated, a coal mine explosion killed 175 men. The highly publicized accident of 1958 killed 74 miners. Many other accidents have punctuated the town's history. Simple monuments scattered throughout the town bear witness to the lives lost bleeding the cold, black, serpentine veins. Few families were untouched, and no generation was without its tombstones.

"They were rough men in a way," writes Ace Foley in his book *The First Fifty Years*, "but beneath that exterior beat a heart of gold. For warmth and friendliness they couldn't be matched. Maybe they didn't have too much in worldly goods, but they were eager to share what they had and every visit there was a delight."

By the 1930s, except for mine accidents, nothing could have troubled the town of 6,400 more than a Fence Buster loss. No community in the nation worshipped its baseball team more than Springhill, where, from the moment they saw their first game, young men dreamed of donning home-town livery. What could matter more in life than being a Buster? There *could* be no more august status. "I've heard it said a dozen times," says first baseman Leo (Sailor) MacDonald, "that Anne Murray doesn't come from Springhill, she comes from the home town of the Springhill Fence Busters." (Recently, a young academic travelled to Springhill to research the working class and the coal mines. However, his work was consistently obstructed by interviewees who insisted on talking first about the Springhill Fence Busters.)

They had reached the provincial semi-finals every year since 1921, winning three Nova Scotia titles and one Maritime championship, and doing it with the crunch of the long ball. On the eve of the Maritime final with the St. Stephen Kiwanis, some were calling the 1933 version the best Busters ever.

They were coached by Jim Conway, a 48-year-old barber who, even on some hot days, sat on the end of the bench wrapped in blankets. Except for two seasons, Conway had coached the Busters since 1922. He was a tough, tactful and sagacious baseball man respected by his players and by the patrons of his barber shop, who would debate baseball strategy unceasingly. Even visiting players dropped by to engage in the amiable discourse.

The 1933 Busters were a balanced unit, but the team forte was pitching. Copie LeBlanc and right-hander Stu McLeod were Maritime mound masters, while self-titled Edgar (The Great) Cormier and theology student Eugene Davis were the equals of many opposing aces. The legal drinking age being 21, half of the Busters' "Million Dollar Infield" were too young to buy a drink— second baseman Lawson Fowler and Leo (Sailor) MacDonald were both 20, while shortstop Jack Fraser was just 22. Veterans in the outfield included Big Bill Wilson, Ackie Albon, also a pitcher of repute, and James (Hank) O'Rourke, the "Babe Ruth of the Maritimes."

The extravagant mythology that encased Springhill-born Hank O'Rourke seemed more veracious because of his appearance. He was a divine creation blessed with a godlike, handsome face atop a six-foot, one-inch frame that supported 190 pounds of marbled muscle. He had cat reflexes and deer swiftness. Only the voice was imperfect. "It was like a hoarsy throat," remembers Sailor MacDonald. "But he had a roar like a porcupine."

The Babe Ruth of the Maritimes, as teammates and reporters dubbed him, was barely out of his teens when his obvious talent forced the Fence Busters' great catcher Brownie Burden into the outfield. Handed the tools of ignorance, O'Rourke immediately tossed aside the chest protector—scorning such protection in a man's game—rolled his socks down to his ankles and caught for 15 years. He was a drawing card province-wide, and with every Fence Buster visit, the folklore was embellished.

One day in Stellarton, Nova Scotia, so part of the legend goes, O'Rourke, hit two home runs and approached the plate once more.

Confidently, he announces to coach Jim Conway, "I'm gonna hit another one."

"C'mon, Hank," says Conway.

"See that white house?" O'Rourke continues.

Conway nods.

"Well, I'm gonna drop one right down the flue."

The fable's last scene has some fellow plucking a baseball out of his chimney.

Another often-told story has as its components a large audience in Halifax, O'Rourke calling his shot, hearing the derision, then clouting the ball over the fence.

"Hank was an entertainer," says MacDonald. "People loved to see him perform. He'd give them all they wanted. He drew people to him, he captivated them. He could hit bullets. And he didn't strike out very often. Every pitcher in the province had respect for him."

One O'Rourke victim was Bobby Brown, later a star with the National League's Boston Braves but at one time a member of the Westville Miners. In a tight game, lore maintains, O'Rourke yanked Brown's fastball into another county. Legends can do that sort of thing.

MacDonald says that O'Rourke was a great storyteller who could elaborate on a funny tale until people laughed twice as hard. He may have acquired that skill at work, among the miners, where he served as an international union representative.

Still, his reputation sometimes made him a target. One summer night after a playoff game in Liverpool, a few Springhill players were singing for a large crowd in front of the Mersey Hotel. O'Rourke was not one of the singers, but he had strolled out of the hotel for cigarettes and was returning to his room when his path was suddenly blocked by Liverpool catcher George Page.

Without a word, the drunken Page reared back and slapped O'Rourke across the face.

The singing stopped, and the crowd stepped back. Some ran.

O'Rourke was still, his eyes glaring into Page's.

"George turned 20 different colors," says Liverpool pitcher Laurie Thorborne. "I thought to myself, 'Oh-oh, we're done.' Christ, Hank could have killed him. I ran right up and I said, 'Hank, let me apologize for the town.' Hank looked at me and said, 'Just let it slide. I'll see him when he's sober. And make him apologize to me.'"

The next day, Page apologized.

While his reputation withstood age, by 1933 O'Rourke's body had faltered. He was now a 34-year-old miner with a weakened throwing arm and failing eyesight about to play the most cunning opponents of his career.

◆ ◆ ◆ ◆

The Maritime final opened in mid-October in St. Stephen on an idyllic afternoon as more than 1,200 customers watched Kiwanis ace Roy Boles duel Springhill's Copie LeBlanc. Down 2-1 in the bottom of the seventh, St. Stephen filled the bases with two out. In an attempt to keep the rally alive, the Kiwanis' George Purcell then lofted a lazy high fly to centre fielder Ackie Albon.

"Albon for years one of the greatest outfielders in the Maritime Provinces was guilty of baseball's gravest error," scolded Ace Foley the next day, "playing an easy catch too cheaply."

The ball fell at his feet, and two runs scored.

Kiwanis won 3-2.

"With two men out, I was giving the man a lot of room and I was playing him as deep as hell," recalls Albon. "And this fella hits a pop fly over second base and—foolish me—I went for the ball. An ordinary outfielder would have played the ball on the bounce. So I go for the ball, and the contour of the ground in back of second is rolling, and that didn't help a damn bit. I could have caught it but the ball hit me in the lower part of the glove. So I picked the ball up and threw it to Copie LeBlanc, and the fella coming home was three or four feet from home plate, and the catcher [O'Rourke] dropped the ball."

While O'Rourke's error was virtually overlooked by the press and forgiven by his teammates, some Fence Busters suspected Albon had purposely fumbled the fly ball because he disliked the haughty LeBlanc. "That was not it at all," insists Albon, "but they really gave me the cold shoulder for a while. You could really feel it."

Game two produced another adroitly pitched effort. Springhill right-hander Stu McLeod yielded three hits to tie the series and beat St. Stephen's Mike Calder 2-0, the latter smitten with the daughter of Fence Busters' coach Conway. Both runs scored in the first inning.

It was a virtuoso performance for McLeod, who was the target of bell-clanging and jeering by Kiwanis fans with an apparently scant appreciation for ritual. Coolly, the pitcher would stroll behind the mound, take out his handkerchief, wipe his brow, stuff the handkerchief back in his pocket, remove his cap, check the inside, place his cap back on, tug it down just right, take out a plug of chewing tobacco, bite off a chew and jam the plug back into his pocket. And he would spit—twice. Amid the jeering and the clanging and the razzing and the spitting, he would walk slowly back to the mound and deliver the next pitch.

Two days later, back in Springhill, the Fence Busters won game three 5-3 before 1,500 fans to move into the series lead. Taking the measure of Howdy Clark and his Nothin' Ball, Copie LeBlanc, in frigid temperatures, permitted just five Kiwanis hits, while the Fence Busters committed six errors.

One of them was a throwing error by Hank O'Rourke, whose eyesight was now so bad that he could barely see past the pitcher's mound. Immediately after his mistake O'Rourke turned towards Conway. It was a silent call of desperation, and the message was received. In a few seconds, eager Artie Crawford stood at O'Rourke's side. The veteran passed his mask to Crawford, in his early 20s, and walked off the field. O'Rourke heard no ovations that day, and no one in the bleachers was inspired to fable. What remained for the Babe Ruth of the Maritimes was a section of the players' bench—and no regrets.

Game four in Springhill was slated for October 20 but was rained out. Rain prohibited play the following day as well. St. Stephen management requested that game four and, if required, game five be combined into a double-header. Fearing lost gate receipts, the

Fence Busters insisted game four be played as a single game. This position would, in the end, hurt the Springhill cause. But for the moment the Busters savored their lead, counted their money and believed what the newspapers said.

The *Chronicle*'s Ace Foley noted that no team had ever won the Maritime provinces amateur baseball championship three years in succession. "The Kiwanis have a chance this season, but from where we sit it looks like a slim chance indeed," Foley wrote.

However slim, the Kiwanis won game four 3-1 on October 22— tying the series behind the sparkling six-hitter of Roy Boles. The loser was Edgar (The Great) Cormier. With their team facing elimination in game four, hundreds of fans back in St. Stephen had milled outside the office of the *Saint Croix Courier*, where the result of each inning was posted in the lower window and a volunteer shouted descriptive accounts from the second floor. In addition, the *Courier* offered a telephone update service that received 600 calls during the game.

It rained the next day, postponing the deciding contest and bringing to nine the number of rained-out playoff games that year in Springhill. Although skies cleared by game time, the diamond was a quagmire. Nearly 200 St. Stephen fans, many of them in town since October 18, walked away exasperated. Some returned home to work—an enviable inconvenience in 1933—but many others stayed, too.

"There were people here from Pictou and Halifax and all over," says Sailor MacDonald, the Fence Busters' first baseman. "Our accommodations were very few, really. The St. Stephen players stayed at the Hyatt Hotel on Main Street. The people that came with them were sleepin' on the floor and every place else. There was some drinkin'—no sense sayin' there was none—but they were orderly. It's pretty hard with people on vacation and with the ballplayers, too."

Recalls Orville Mitchell: "One day, we were waitin' to play a game and a team of horses came up the road. We had a big rooting section there, and there was really nothing for them to do around town, so they formed a little parade. They walked way down to Westville and then had to march back up that hill. And there was this old fella all alone with his horse and wagon. All those people went with him. And Abe Prilutsky [an avid fan] crawled in up alongside him and drove the horses up the front street, and we were all marching in behind, headed up towards the liquor store. We didn't have any money and weren't goin' in, but the guy in the store didn't know this. He took a look and panicked and locked the door."

People found various ways to pass the time. Roy Boles relays a tale of ladies' man Laurie Crompton, the pitcher who was Boles' roommate in Springhill. "It was just him and I in the room when this girl came in—she was goin' to make the beds. Laurie got playin' up to her ... and I left. He got this babe there to stay with him. Stayed right there. He said he made out all right with her."

It rained again October 24. This time, however, the Kiwanis could wait no longer. Arriving with $1,300, the team left for home with no money and without an agreement on a rubber game.

"It was raining so bad that, on the way back, we had to take a side road from Moncton to Saint John," says Mitchell. "We went over a bridge, and Bill McIntosh got out to see if the planks were still all there. And just as soon as Charlie Godfrey goes over in his taxi, jeez, away goes all the planks. That washed it out right there."

Long-distance negotiations commenced the next day, and from the outset these sessions were as antagonistic as the games. The Kiwanis proposed that game five happen on the first fine day and on neutral ground. They suggested Moncton—160 miles from St. Stephen and 60 miles from Springhill. No, said the Fence Busters, it's Springhill on October 30 or nothing.

The next day the Fence Busters sent a telegram to the Kiwanis insisting that they return the 220 miles to Springhill immediately. The Kiwanis said they would come, provided that they were guaranteed $400, rain or shine. Again the Fence Busters said no. "The guarantee sought is beyond any reason," Springhill manager Conway told the Saint John *Telegraph-Journal.*

The Maritime Provinces Branch of the Amateur Athletic Union of Canada, ultimately responsible for the series, was nearly invisible during the struggle. Incredibly, the issue was raised only "informally" at the annual athletic union meeting on October 25 in Amherst, Nova Scotia. If the matter came to the branch, president Charles Gillespie intoned, it would go before the executive for a vote. "If the teams want to play and declare a championship—and it seems like they want to—then it rests entirely with the heads of both clubs to come to an agreement. The M.P.B. cannot force the teams to play baseball. In fact, the branch will take no further steps in the matter unless it is absolutely necessary."

Exactly what would have constituted an absolute necessity is difficult to imagine.

So on October 28 the negotiations picked up once more. St. Stephen offered to return to Springhill, and slashed the monetary guarantee it would need from $400 to $200. Again, the Fence Busters said no.

By the next morning the entire debate seemed moot because the mining town was blanketed in snow. On October 30 the athletic union issued a sonorous proclamation warning that if the teams did not settle within "a reasonable time," the organization would declare no winner that year.

Meanwhile, back in St. Stephen, it was decided to try again to salvage the series. Realizing that the Moncton diamond was now unfit and that both Saint John and St. Stephen diamonds were playable, the Kiwanis presented three options: play in Springhill with a $200 guarantee; play in Saint John and split expenses; play in St. Stephen with the Fence Busters taking 100 percent of the gate, minus the umpire's fee. The Kiwanis would pay for the advertising. The Fence Busters nixed all three options. A. J. Mason, president of the Springhill Amateur Athletic Association, was terse in his respsonse: "Springhill executive stands pat. Will post no guarantee."

The refusal of Springhill to make even a minute compromise exasperated Kiwanis management and fuelled the rumor that the Fence Busters so feared Roy Boles that they were prepared to kill the series rather than be beaten a third time by the right-handed ace. Unwilling to let the Busters slip away, the citizens' committee collected approximately $200 from St. Stephen merchants, and on October 31 the Kiwanis relented and agreed to play in Springhill two days later, November 2. Failing that, the next day, November 3. They demanded no monetary guarantee.

Springhill management had cleanly out-negotiated the Kiwanis, but it was a Pyrrhic victory. "Our fellas never worked out or nothing," says Springhill second baseman Lawson Fowler. "I said, 'They'll never come here.' A lot of them thought it was pretty well over. We never even had a ball in our hands, never practised. Copie [LeBlanc] went back to Moncton."

Kiwanis centre fielder Gordon Coffey smiles as he recalls: "We kept on practising [while] we were trying to schedule that fifth game. For practices we had to get the fellas off work at three o'clock because it was dark at six o'clock that time of year. And we kept that up in the hope that we would get the game in."

In the early morning of November 1, with $200 in their kitty and a Million Dollar Infield in their sights, the Kiwanis pulled out of St. Stephen. They arrived in Springhill late that night, confident in Boles but largely ignorant of their enormous preparatory advantage.

In Springhill, it was widely known that the Fence Busters had retired their bats on October 24, the day the Kiwanis had left town. At least one opportunistic resident attempted to turn this rust to gold.

◆　◆　◆　◆

Roy Boles awakened early on the sun-soaked Springhill morning of November 2. But he didn't get up right away. Instead, he lay in bed in his hotel room thinking about home, where, in a few hours, people would crowd in front of the *Courier* office to scrutinize the windows for the inning-by-inning scores. The fans would cheer and groan and bounce up and down to keep warm, and they would anticipate and even pray. Some really did pray, Boles knew. On his broad shoulders and in his right arm rested the answers to those prayers. He lay back and looked at the ceiling for a few more minutes.

Around nine o'clock, someone rapped on his door.

In his stocking feet and only partially dressed, Boles opened the door and gazed at a man about 40 years old.

"Your name Boles?" he asked.

"Yeah," Boles said.

"You're pitchin' today?"

With this, the stranger walked into the room. Boles immediately noticed his smooth voice and expensive suit and how he seemed to carry himself like a successful businessman. Boles permitted himself a quick fantasy about a major league contract about to be pulled from the stranger's pocket.

The stranger was all smiles. Boles was smiling, too, but the ballplayer was rapidly becoming uneasy about this mystery.

Then the man reached inside of his coat and pulled out an

envelope. It was closed but not sealed. "There's $2,000 in here," he said. "I'll give ya $2,000."

Boles stood silent. His smile faded.

The stranger waited a few seconds for a reaction—another smile, a wink, a nod, a thank-you, anything. The stranger's smile was fading, too. And the silence seemed to be making him edgy.

"Do you know what I'm givin' you $2,000 for?"

Still nothing.

"You're pitchin' today, ain't ya?"

The stranger extended his arm, holding the envelope inches from Boles. "Then here."

"Take your $2,000," said Boles, his voice icy, "and get the hell out of here."

The stranger looked cautiously at Boles, put the envelope back into his pocket and closed the door behind him.

At 2 p.m. on Friday, November 2, the improbable game commenced in improbable sunshine before more than 1,100 paying spectators. It quickly became apparent that is was not going to be much of a contest. St. Stephen cracked four runs in the second inning off LeBlanc, then added another four in the fourth. Before the hemorrhaging stopped, it was 13-2. Gordon Coffey and first baseman Ray Jellison went three-for-five, and Boles permitted just seven hits. Springhill, looking clumsy and inept, committed five errors. It was an excruciating exhibition for the players and the spectators and anyone associated with this noble team. In a few cases, the chagrin turned to anger.

"We arrived back at the hotel," recalls Boles, "and I got out of the car to walk across the street and [Fence Busters manager Jim] Conway's daughter got out and called me all the names she could think of. She wasn't drunk, just mad. It was embarrassing for me and embarrassing for all the players. She's calling me all kinds of names and everybody in the street's lookin' and wonderin' what's goin' on. I just walked into the hotel and didn't say nothin'. I couldn't figure out what she was calling me all these names for. She said, 'If it wasn't for you, you son of a bitch, we would have won.'"

The next day, the Kiwanis returned home to celebrations that were developing into annual events: a 150-car parade, flags, bunting, banquets, bands and a myriad of speeches from the verandah of the biggest hotel in the happiest little town in the Dominion. More than 1,500 fans braved a cold wind to cheer Gordon Coffey as he hoisted high the McLellan Cup, presented to the team for winning three straight Maritime senior baseball championships.

Back in Springhill, it snowed.

THE YEAR THE BRAVES CAME TO TOWN

"Christ, don't kill anybody out there today."
—A Boston Braves coach—

THEY ARRIVED in the late evening, through a sticky drizzle, still in uniform from a lethargic win 100 miles south in the minor metropolis of Bangor, Maine. Few of the Boston Braves, financially strapped also-rans of the National League, enjoyed these mid-summer safaris to the edge of civilization. But in 1934, when management said go, players went. So the weary, forlorn team travelled northward to St. Stephen, New Brunswick, to toy with amateurs for $1,000 up front, guaranteed rain or shine. They would also receive a percentage of the gate, free accommodations and free advertising.

Tomorrow, on a dirt diamond encircled by a race track, they would play the local heroes, the champions of Maritime senior baseball for three years running. But this was hardly in the forefront of their minds as they yawned and alighted one by one from the bus and plodded into the finest of everything that the aging but proud Queen Hotel could offer. Eventually the guests changed clothes and ate and mingled with townspeople who had tiptoed into the lobby to ogle the weary deities with familiar names and uncommon skills: Fred Frankhouse, "Jumbo" Jim Elliott, Pinkey Whitney and Wally Berger.

"I talked with them a bit, so I really wasn't in awe," says Kiwanis playing coach Orville Mitchell, "but I know a lot of people were in awe."

What a strange man Len Webber was for suggesting that the Kiwanis challenge professionals, major leaguers at that. Some people had expressed concern that the match would result in embarrassment for the town. The conservative, rake-thin secretary Webber—always toting a little bag with money in it, always smoking his pipe, always calm and attentive to detail—knew, however, that there was a time to roll the dice. And this was a colossal gamble.

The Kiwanis were already $500 in the hole, and a $1,000 rain-out would drown the team, ending baseball at least for the season and perhaps for the rest of the decade. And so far the summer of '34 had been miserable—chilly, rainy and damp. As game day approached, Webber must have peered skyward and prayed. A lot.

He need not have prayed for community support. Immediately after the initial organizational meeting, held in a church vestry, rumor of the Braves' visit swept through town. Long before it was official, the 500-seat grandstand sold out at $2.50 a head—10 times the usual price. The idea set the town afloat, and talk on the street was of little else. Some townsfolk even speculated about whether the Kiwanis could beat the perennially feeble—and likely overconfident—National Leaguers.

Despite the fact that most major league teams considered these moderately profitable exhibitions to be indignities, the Braves had promised to field their best players. Knowing this, the *Saint Croix Courier* admonished that the Kiwanis were merely "a community team ... [and] this game is not expected to be hotly contested by any means." Still, fans could dream, couldn't they?

◆ ◆ ◆ ◆

The St. Croix Valley was infatuated with anything Bostonian. The Massachusetts capital and the Maritime provinces were bonded by historical and social links influencing everything from architecture to accent. For generations Maritimers had jaunted to "the Boston States" to nibble the erudite city they considered more alluring than Montreal or Toronto.

It was a two-way trade. Charles F. Adams, a wealthy Boston businessman and part owner of the Braves and the Boston Bruins of the National Hockey League, maintained a fishing camp near Boiestown, New Brunswick, on the shores of the Miramichi River. Here, Adams hosted New England aristocracy such as Peter Blodgett, of the First National Bank of Boston. Eastern Steamship Lines ran *The Saint John* between the two cities. "Everywhere I go I learn about my friends and their friends who are planning fishing trips to New Brunswick," wrote Eastern president Alton B. Sharp.

In sports, several young American ballplayers, including the Boston Braves' Bobby Brown, played Maritime senior baseball during the first half of the century. In the 1870s and 1880s the flow had been in the other direction, with young Maritimers seeking work and play in New England. Recently, it is probably not coincidental that Donald Sweeney, the first St. Stephen native to star in the NHL, is a Boston Bruin.

If their spotty record did not exactly instill awe, the Braves could at least point to their status as an original National League team. In the years since the league's birth in 1876, the Braves' successes had been few. Between 1917 and 1932 they had finished in the first half of the standings just once. Perhaps not surprisingly, they ran a distant second financially to their affluent American League cousins, the Boston Red Sox. Throughout the 1930s the Braves neared bankruptcy, an ironic fate given that the first Braves owner, Arthur Soden, once proclaimed, "Common sense tells me that baseball is played primarily to make a profit."

In 1934 this eclectic tribe of has-beens would rally to finish a respectable fourth among eight teams, 16 games behind the St. Louis Cardinals' Gas House Gang. In any case, the Braves were governed by two rules: 1) Show up for games on time, and 2) stay out of jail. Even these ordinances were enforced selectively.

With an average age of 32, the Braves had the oldest pitching staff in the league. The best pitcher was Fred Frankhouse, 30, a curve-baller. The biggest was six-foot-three, 235-pound "Jumbo" Jim Elliott, 33. The youngest was Bobby Brown, 23, who had thrown for the Westville Miners in 1929. The oddest was Dick (Kewpie) Barrett, a 28-year-old average right-hander who for two seasons called himself Dick Oliver. As Dick Barrett, he would pitch the final two innings against the Kiwanis. The Braves' starter in St. Stephen would be veteran Leo (Blackie) Mangum, 38.

Defensively, the team was bland, although Arthur (Pinkey) Whitney, 29, was a superb third baseman. Offensively, Boston lacked home-run power but hit reasonably well. First baseman Buck Jordan led with a .311 average.

Amid all of this mediocrity were three gems: the manager, the slugger and the Rabbit.

Manager Bill (Deacon Bill) McKechnie was a strange choice to lead such a tawdry brood. Raised in a religious home, McKechnie spoke softly, lived cleanly, never drank, and sang in the same choir for a quarter century. Rare indeed was this professional ballplayer with warm eyes and an allaying smile. Clearly, the Braves' ownership realized that in McKechnie they had a superior human being and an astute baseball mind, one that could wring from his players the full extent of their skills. Before he was finished, McKechnie would win pennants with three National League teams—a record.

The Braves' pre-eminent attraction was 29-year-old Chicagoan Wally Berger. A good-looking blond outfielder, Berger was Boston's only *bona fide* star, and in the mid-1930s he was one of the game's leading home run hitters. He played in all of the team's 152 games in 1934, batting in 121 runs and hitting 34 homers. All other Braves combined had just 49 home runs. In 11 seasons he homered 242 times, a lofty sum given his weak supporting cast.

The team's boldest affront to convention was a 43-year-old Massachusetts native named James Walter Vincent Maranville, the Rabbit. The five-foot-five Rabbit, so called because of his hippity-hoppity movements and his large ears, played 2,670 major league games, came to bat more than 10,000 times and hit a lifetime .258. For his statistics, he would enter the Hall of Fame. For his mirth, he would become a legend.

Maranville, who travelled with a pet monkey, once disguised himself in blackface and delivered a profane singing telegram to his manager. In Boston, he swam across the Charles River to avoid walking 10 blocks. In St. Louis, he dove into a fountain on a dare and emerged with a goldfish in his mouth. In Philadelphia, teammates locked him in his hotel room so they could commence a quiet game of cards, but Maranville escaped by crawling out of his 12th-floor window. In New York, he chased a teammate down the street yelling, "Stop, thief!" From time to time Maranville consumed too much booze and would be asked to sleep it off overnight at the police station—a scenario that seemed to satisfy his wife. "At least I know where he is," she said.

◆ ◆ ◆ ◆

Tuesday, July 17, 1934, dawned a magnificent bright, clear and dewy-soft morning befitting the glorious event. St. Stephen and Milltown, New Brunswick, had proclaimed a public holiday from one o'clock to five o'clock that afternoon, Calais merchants gave their employees all afternoon off, and virtually every store and factory on the border closed. Soon cars from afar jammed Water and King streets in what was to be St. Stephen's largest influx of people ever. "The crowds on the streets and the presence of the inevitable balloon peddler were reminiscent of the days when the traveling circus was an Annual Event in the life of a small town," reported the *Saint Croix Courier.* Reporters from Boston and throughout the Maritimes converged.

No naked plain was ever more resplendent than St. Stephen's dirt diamond in the middle of a race track. The flag pole in centre field seemed almost phosphorescent with its fresh coat of white paint. Lines on the base paths were straight and bright. Temporary fences sprouted in the outfield, 325 feet down the base lines—a major league distance. Even the horse stalls gleamed.

The teams followed the Calais marching band onto the exhibition grounds. The press estimated that 5,000 people engulfed the diamond that day, but Orville Mitchell says the guess was low. "The guy selling tickets at the gate went to watch the game," he says. "We lost a good many hundreds of dollars right there because the people were still coming in. And others sneaked through the back woods, the fellas that couldn't pay a dollar" in general admission.

Initially the Braves were taken aback with the St. Stephen facility. "That diamond was lightning fast," says Mitchell, "and before they started, they were told, 'Christ, don't kill anybody out there today.' If they hit a ball at somebody, they were likely to blow their head off. They worried about the pitcher —hittin' him and hurtin' him."

The teams stood caps over hearts as the Calais band clattered out *The Star Spangled Banner.* (It is unclear whether *O Canada* or *God Save the King* was also played.) The secretary of the Maritime Provinces Branch of the Amateur Athletic Union of Canada, Charles C. Gillespie, natty and political as usual, introduced the players to polite applause, then lofted the ceremonial first pitch.

On the sidelines Bill McKechnie Jr., the Boston manager's son who would play briefly in the game, smiled at this exuberant rural theatre. He noticed that the tedium carried into town the night before was gone from the faces of his teammates. "It's sometimes hard to get the boys enthusiastic in their regular league games, but when they come on a trip like this and realize that some of the people there in the stands have travelled a hundred miles or more just to see them play, it means something," he would tell the press after the game.

To ensure interest from the United States side of the border, the Kiwanis had injected a few extra American players into their line-up.

One of them was Joe Lydic, a lithe first baseman from Woodland, Maine, about 10 miles from St. Stephen. Another was Hank Hamilton, an able and experienced catcher from Calais. But the showcased player was an easy-going 16-year-old Calais native named Kenny Kallenberg.

Kallenberg was the starting pitcher, although Kiwanis manager Mitchell thought it unfair that regular pitchers Roy Boles, Mike Calder and newly acquired Cecil (Lefty) Brownell should yield the honor to the teenager. But his objections fell limp. The citizens' committee that controlled team finances wanted Kallenberg. The choice certainly pleased several professional scouts who had arrived to assess the youngster. No doubt the same scouts also influenced the decision. "They wanted the Braves to look Kallenberg over good," says Boles. "I know that Brownell was mad, and I know that Calder was mad. They should have put the kid in the last part."

Kallenberg had only learned the previous day that he would be starting, and as game time grew near, so did his terror. "I was scared out of my wits. I didn't even feel my feet touching the ground. I didn't walk out [onto the field], I floated. The hair was standing up on the back of my neck out there. I was pretty much dazed ... I had never seen them before. We had no television and I had never seen a major league baseball game. I used to hear them on the radio— these guys were heroes to me. There was a helluva crowd and I was wondering myself what was going to happen. Whatever it was, I was hoping that it happened quick."

It did.

Braves lead-off hitter Tommy Thompson doubled, moved to second on Marty McManus's infield out, then scored on Randy Moore's single. Still, Kallenberg slipped out of the inning after having allowed just the one run. But following St. Stephen's three-up, three-down first inning, Kallenberg strolled to the mound to die 5,000 deaths—one for every fan who winced in sympathy.

The second inning began well enough, with Kallenberg striking out the great Pinkey Whitney. He then surrendered four consecutive hits before getting the second out. Appearing to lose all composure, he hit slugger Wally Berger with a pitch. The fans murmured. He balked in a run. Mumbles turned to boos as the cruel assault on a schoolboy's dream continued. A third run crossed, then another and another. In all, the Braves had 10 hits and scored eight runs. Kallenberg finished the inning, turned his back on the carnage and repaired solemnly to the Kiwanis bench. The crowd was silent. The score was 9-0.

"After it was over I didn't feel like hangin' around," Kallenberg remembers. "I felt a little bit foolish. I mean, I didn't figure I was gonna pitch a no-hitter or anything, but Christ ... I felt like I just wanted to get the hell out of there."

Lefty Brownell, who that year joined the team after starring in Saint John, pitched the third inning. Brownell, too, had a memorable moment, beginning when Braves manager McKechnie pulled over his star player, Berger, and whispered something about now being the time. So with two out and the bases empty, Berger strutted to the plate—an exemplary athlete in his absolute prime.

Brownell delivered a fastball. Berger uncoiled—a compact, graceful and efficient swing. Softly the ball arched over the temporary outfield fencing as 10,000 eyes marvelled at its flight. Never mind that a pre-game ground rule netted Berger only second base. This was a Home Run!

Over his shoulder, Brownell glanced at the major league king standing casually in the middle of the diamond in the late afternoon sun.

"He teed off on me and I don't think I have ever heard anything sound so nice," recalls the pitcher. "Oh, man. I swear that the thing landed in St. George [40 miles away]. He flattened 'er right out, I swear."

Brownell got the next batter on a ground ball, stranding the great Berger on second base and capping the game's most storied stanza.

With the outcome assured and the home side no longer paralyzed with wonderment, the Kiwanis relaxed and swung freely at Leo Mangum, the Braves' starting pitcher. The result was intriguing.

Second baseman Bill McIntosh began the inning with the Kiwanis' first hit of the game, a single over the head of shortstop Dan McGee. Brownell then reached base on a fielder's choice. The Kiwanis' new right fielder Earl (Squirrelly) Ross doubled, sending Brownell to third. Orville Mitchell, who had replaced young Lydic in the inning, looped a double into centre field, scoring both Brownell and Ross as the grandstand bounced with glee. Nine-two. Mitchell subsequently scored the third and final run of the inning when Rainnie Moffatt singled to right. Nine-three.

The Braves touched Brownell for two more runs in the fourth, but he blanked the fifth inning, finishing his stint with four hits over three innings. Roy Boles worked the sixth and seventh inning, facing just seven men in the two innings and yielding only one hit.

As he watched this unexpected home-town magic, Orville Mitchell felt a tap on his shoulder. An acquaintance nodded at the ball basket near the Kiwanis bench. Mitchell gulped. They were running out of baseballs! The embarrassing spectre of Kiwanis players begging patrons to return their souvenirs floated through his mind. The playing-coach turned ashen.

"We had six dozen balls for that game, and that would ordinarily last us for an entire season," he says. "I didn't realize that they were going to rope off the outfield. And every time you hit a two-bagger in the crowd, you lost the ball. With all the foul balls that were being hit, we were down to less than a dozen balls."

Mitchell desperately scanned the crowd and spotted a friend who worked in a Calais sporting goods store. The friend was quickly dispatched to retrieve all of the balls he had in stock. That turned out to be only a dozen or so, but enough to complete the game.

Meanwhile, Mike Calder inherited the mound from Boles and held Boston hitless over the final two innings. Calder struck out three and made a bare-handed stop in the ninth, tossing the ball to Mitchell at first base for an easy out.

The final score was 11-3.

It could have been—and likely should have been—worse.

"The 'pures' put up a much better argument than the semi-pros of Bangor," wrote Joe Cashman, of the *Boston Herald*.

The game raised $2,952.97, from which the Braves claimed $1,140. After expenses and repayment to creditors, the Kiwanis were left with more than $1,200—a tidy sum that turned a $500 deficit into a $700 balance, just as Webber had planned.

In all, 14 Braves and 15 Kiwanis played. Boston had 15 hits, the Kiwanis 10—Squirrelly Ross, Muddy McLain, Rainnie Moffatt and Bill McIntosh collecting two hits each. Four errors were committed, all of them by St. Stephen. The game lasted an hour and 33 minutes, about half of the time it takes to complete a modern major league game.

Through the swamp of numbers, however, one statistical extract has floated for half a century. Over the last seven innings—when the Kiwanis' starting line-up was on the field, when the regular pitchers were on the mound, when the team relaxed—the score was St. Stephen Kiwanis 3, Boston Braves 2.

◆ ◆ ◆ ◆

In the spring of 1934, before the Braves' visit, the Kiwanis had entered their exhibition season with a few changes. A member of the Kiwanis executive, Bill Whitlock, was elected president of the New Brunswick Amateur Baseball Association. Second baseman Mitchell became the coach, replacing Art Middlemiss, who resigned because of work commitments with his candy-making employer, Ganong Bros. The arrival of outfielder Squirrelly Ross gave the team a swift runner, a competent hitter and an irrepressible scamp.

But the big catch was Lefty Brownell, a southpaw from Saint John, giving the Kiwanis a surfeit of good pitchers. Mike Calder was used infrequently, although his size and fastball made him a professional prospect. Howdy Clark, an original Mohawk, could start or relieve.

Roy Boles, at season's outset still recognized as the ace pitcher, endured a troubled summer, seldom playing. When he did pitch, he looked weak, gaunt and unsure.

Boles had contracted scarlet fever in the spring, as had most of the members of his family. Quarantined in his room, he grew despondent. "Time passes slowly when one is kept indoors these fine days," wrote the *Courier*. "[So] if some admirer of the smartest baseball pitcher and the sweetest pinch hitter these provinces have produced in recent years would loan him a radio, he would be most grateful. One day last fall in Springhill Roy could have had a dozen radios from frantic fans just for the asking."

A day after this appeal Boles heard a voice outside of his window telling him to get a rope and lower it to the street. The ailing athlete did as instructed. In a few moments Boles leaned out of his window and hauled the rope back into his room. On the end of the rope was tied ... a radio.

Despite the loss of Boles, the Kiwanis had a strong season and practically drew a bye into the 1934 provincial final. Meanwhile, eight other New Brunswick teams battled in four series.

The Kiwanis easily defeated their lone foe, the St. Stephen Blue

Caps—the town's erstwhile intermediate club that in years past had been used by the Kiwanis as an unofficial farm team. Grasping for some credibility, the Blue Caps had registered masochistically this season in the senior baseball category. They would not make the mistake twice, next season moving back to the intermediate level.

In the provincial final the Kiwanis beat Saint John YMCI in four games. Recovered from his illness, Boles pitched 11 innings in game one, yielded just six hits and slugged a grand slam home run in the 12th inning. The teams split games two and three. Then in the fourth and deciding game, rotund Charlie Godfrey drove in five runs and scored twice in an 8-4 victory that capped St. Stephen's fourth straight New Brunswick title. (Godfrey had again replaced injured Muddy McLain, who had stepped in a hole, crashed into some wire, twisted his ankle and ended his season.)

Meanwhile, in Yarmouth, Nova Scotia, the Gateways parallelled the Kiwanis' addition of Brownell by annexing their own left-handed ace, Copie LeBlanc. With the Springhill Fence Busters in 1933 and with Halifax and Moncton before that, 23-year-old LeBlanc was widely believed to be Nova Scotia's top pitcher. Maybe even the best in the Maritimes. Certainly, LeBlanc believed so, and it showed. "He was a good player, but he wasn't the best," says Boles, who played with LeBlanc in Moncton in 1930. "He hated everybody. Nobody liked him, either."

The Gateways were circumspect about LeBlanc. "I admired his ability," concedes veteran pitcher Nate Bain, "but not his personality or his way of life. But when we got into the game, he was accepted as a member of the team."

Dividends were immediate as LeBlanc led the Gateways to the 1934 Nova Scotia title.

Behind LeBlanc and Bain were two talented youngsters: Ken Venoit and fireballing Purney Fuller, who was just five-foot-two. But the Gateways had more than good pitching that season. The infield and the outfield were both solid. It featured Red Goudey in centre, who in his teens had learned to play his position while living near Boston. Lead-off hitter Edgar (Lightning) Amirault played in left, and Murray Veno was in right.

Murray (Papa) Veno began as a catcher but by the mid-1930s was courageously calling himself an outfielder—a troublesome description for purists. "He was a rather uncertain [outfielder] because he would usually overrun the ball and then have to backtrack to make the catch in rather exciting fashion," Halifax sports columnist Ace Foley would write years later.

A superior hitter on the First World War Canadian army team that once upset the powerful United States army team, the short and nimble Veno played into the 1940s with military teams and provincial amateur teams, subsequently coaching for two decades.

"Murray was a ballplayer's ballplayer," says teammate Nate Bain. "It didn't matter if you were five runs ahead or five runs behind, Murray always played for one more."

Veno's flare and unfading grin endeared him to all. Bouncing, crashing, diving, stealing, sliding and always hustling. (Once, during an old-timers' game, 78-year-old Veno came to bat and was hit by a pitch. Several hundred spectators gasped. Veno, however, merely dusted himself off and smiled. "That's one way to get on base," he said.)

Zest aside, Veno is forever recalled for an ostentatious stunt that he performed over and over to the delight of audiences across the region. Not content simply to score a run, he adorned it, propelled it to another level of entertainment and personalized it. A fleet runner, he would race down the third base line, turn a complete somersault in mid-air and land with both feet on home plate. He never missed. Crowds awaited the moment, Veno awaited their reaction.

Teammates did not resent his showmanship; in fact, many were inspired by his unorthodox ways. Once, in Charlottetown, Veno was berating Gateways' star shortstop Halley Horton for not coming through with a hit in a key situation. In mid-lecture he was cut off by Doug Horton, Halley's older and much larger brother.

"C'mon, Murray," said Doug Horton, casting a dark shadow over Veno. "There's no need in havin' a fight over this."

Veno stopped and looked up at Doug Horton.

"Well," Veno said with a comedic pause, "considering you are too big for me ... I guess you are right."

In his final years circulation problems would require that Veno have his right leg amputated above the knee. Following the operation, surrounded by flowers of sympathy in his hospital room and facing the rest of his days in a wheelchair, he beamed at a sympathetic visitor.

"Won't be stealing any more bases now," he said.

◆　◆　◆　◆

The surface of the St. Stephen diamond was still slippery and damp from the previous day's rain when the Kiwanis and Gateways limbered up that September before game one of the 1934 Maritime finals.

Midway into the warm-up, talented Gateways catcher Nelson Deveau was struck by an errant throw from the Kiwanis' side of the field. Deveau slumped immediately to his knees and spat out five teeth. "Where the hell are you throwing the ball?" he snapped through the blood. Players from both teams quickly surrounded the fallen catcher, who ended up watching the game from the bleachers, complaining about missing a steak dinner that evening.

Catcher lost, inspiration found.

"The Gateways came to bat with blood in their eye," reported the *Halifax Chronicle*. Yarmouth scored four runs in the first inning, sending Kiwanis starter Roy Boles to the bench with one out and the bases loaded. Lefty Brownell finished the game. But the Gateways' anger could not sustain their attack. St. Stephen battled back to win 12-5.

Down a game, the next day the Gateways started 19-year-old southpaw sensation Purney Fuller, who had struck out 33 batters during a 12-inning high school playoff game earlier that year. Pitted against giant Mike Calder, Fuller—whose boyish face photographed with an enduring up-yours expression—tripped the Kiwanis with sharp curve balls. Still, the Kiwanis won again, this time 3-2.

That night the teams left for Yarmouth in vastly different states of mind. Apart from injured catcher Muddy McLain, the Kiwanis were healthy and resolute. The Gateways, on the other hand, griped about the umpiring, which resulted in Springhill's Bill Noiles replacing Halifax's Frank Martin. The Gateways also commiserated with catcher Deveau, who was returning home with fewer teeth, and with centre fielder Red Goudey, who was sporting a cold compress on his right wrist. Also, LeBlanc and Gateways management had stopped talking to each other. The reasons for this silence were never made clear, but LeBlanc was likely disturbed that he had been passed over in favor of Fuller. Consequently, LeBlanc, perhaps the best pitcher in all of Eastern Canada, and only four months in Gateways blue, would sit on the bench for the rest of the series. It was a death blow.

Still, some Gateways found a way to cope, and none better than third baseman Prescott (Biss) Boyd.

Biss Boyd played baseball, but alcohol played Biss Boyd.

"One game in Springhill that I was pitchin', a ball was winged down to Biss at third," says Nate Bain, "and he got in front of it. But he saw two balls. He finally put his glove down, and Halley Horton came running over saying, 'No, no, it's the other one!' All that Biss did was lean over and pick up the ball and toss it up in the air and say, 'Hey, hey.'"

An employee of Yarmouth North hydro company, 29-year-old Boyd was a talented but inconsistent fielder and a former starter in the local semi-pro league of the mid-1920s. Five-foot-10-inches tall and 150 pounds, Boyd had a narrow face—sad, sluggish and bland. Only his brown eyes, at least in his younger days, were alert and merry.

A photograph taken on a Yarmouth wharf shows virtually the entire Gateway team in suits and ties, except Boyd, who looks like he may have spent the night on the wharf. He wears no tie, a cap at least one size too large is pulled down over his eyes, a belt buckle is askew, and a jacket is pulled back on his shoulders. A cigarette dangles in his hand.

He conspired often with Gateways veteran catcher Pete White, a construction worker, to enliven an otherwise straight-laced team. Brought together, Boyd and White lived in their own booze-sopped, slurred wonderland of Biss 'n Pete.

At their peak they were an inside joke shared by an entire town and by all of Maritime amateur baseball. A Yarmouth police officer as a lark once handcuffed Biss 'n' Pete to ensure that they boarded the team bus on time. Everyone laughed, everyone understood.

Neither loud nor abrasive, Boyd was reared in a solid, middle-class family. But by the mid-1930s he was unhappily married with several children. In this pale existence, only baseball and booze mattered to him, teammates say.

Halley Horton often had Boyd as an overnight house guest to

ensure his reasonable sobriety for a pending game. But that was in Yarmouth. Road games were another matter, rich with possibility and opportunity for Biss 'n Pete.

First baseman Doug Horton recalls an incident that occurred in the Queen Hotel in Halifax. A game was scheduled for that afternoon, and team manager Ed Garson did not want the notorious pair to start drinking. "We were there in the lobby, and Ed thought they might have been into somethin' and Pete was starting out the door—I can still see those revolving doors," Horton says. "Pete would go out the door and the next thing Ed would go chase him and go around the block or somethin'. He'd no sooner get back and get sat down when Biss would get up and go. They really kept Ed going. They had nothing to do."

Another time, Horton and his brother Halley were sitting in a St. Stephen restaurant when a fellow and a girl came in and ordered a meal. "After a while, who should come in but Biss—he never even paid a bit of attention to Halley or I—and sits right down behind this fella and his girl," Doug Horton says. "The waiter came over and took his order, and he ordered a really good meal. Halley turned to me and said that we should get out of here before we get stuck with his cheque. But I said let's stay, so we took our time eatin' our ice cream.

"Now, this fella was being very attentive to his girl, y'know. After Biss gets through, the waiter came over and Biss said, 'Is this cheque for me? I can't pay this. I'm sorry, I haven't got the money.' And the waiter gets quite mad. So Biss starts tellin' him this long cock-and-bull story that he was just makin' up on the spot, about how far he travelled and how he hadn't had anything to eat for such a long time. And he was puttin' on this sob story, and it went so good that the feller with the girl sittin' behind him tapped the waiter on the shoulder and said, 'I'll pay it for him.' He was showin' off in front of his girl, y'see. So he took the cheque, and Biss got up and thanked him very kindly and said that he feels much better now that the meal will be paid for. And he walked out. He never said boo to Halley or I."

Despite his misery, Boyd retained a dignity and a kindness manifested in spontaneous, simple gestures. "One day, I saw him walking up John Street," remembers Halley Horton, "and there was this kid, maybe four or five years old, and she was trying to open this door to get into this apartment. Ol' Biss turned around and looked and came staggering all the way back and opened that door for her. Just somethin' simple, but that was Biss Boyd."

◆   ◆   ◆   ◆

The five days between games two and three of the final healed some Gateway wounds. Centre fielder Red Goudey's wrist recovered, and Nels Deveau could catch if absolutely needed. But the team mood remained generally sombre. Unlike its ailing team, the town of Yarmouth was ebullient. Citizens paraded the Gateways, "as though [the] sturdy men had returned laden with honors," reported Acc Foley. Here, people had not lost faith in the redemptive power of the local boy, and at a popular restaurant the Yarmouth Amateur Athletic Association feted both teams, giving Gateways playing coach Ernie Grimshaw a standing ovation.

More than 2,000 fans witnessed game three, with almost every woman in the park showing her support by wearing blue, the Gateways' team color. After four intense innings young Purney Fuller and Lefty Brownell were deadlocked 1-1. Some Yarmouth fans dared to envision a fourth game and an extended series...until the fifth inning—15 minutes for which Biss Boyd would receive much attention but no mercy.

With St. Stephen's Bill McIntosh on first and no outs, Boyd dropped an easy pop-up at third but recovered in time to get McIntosh going to second for the force out. Still, the flub was an omen.

After Squirrelly Ross walked, Boyd gathered in a ground ball and threw out Orville Mitchell at first. McIntosh and Ross advanced a base.

Then came the critical play.

The Kiwanis' Rainnie Moffatt tapped down to Boyd who blocked the ball, then inexplicably fired it several feet over the head of first baseman Doug Horton, the tallest man on the field. As Horton scrambled after the ball and a tidal wave of derision swept over the infield, three Kiwanis runs scored. St. Stephen won 5-4, capturing their fourth straight Maritime title.

The teams had barely left the field when the beam of scorn shone on Boyd. "The Kiwanis did not deserve today's victory," castigated Ace Foley. "Biss Boyd, veteran third sacker, gave them a gift of three runs in the fifth, on an inexcusable poor throw to first, a throw he had a world of time to make accurate.... That error by Boyd lost the game, the series and the championship.... This department nominates Boyd as the goat of the series."

It had been a bitter series riddled with residual belligerence that bubbled over at odd moments and in odd locations. Roy Boles witnessed a confrontation away from the field involving the Kiwanis' giant pitcher, Mike Calder. "He was sitting there in the front seat of a car [and he] peeled a banana. When he threw the peelin' out, two local guys come over and said, 'What you think this is, a garbage dump around here?' He got out of the car and looked down at them and said, 'What you gonna do about?' They walked away."

The teams attended banquets in each other's towns, but otherwise, cordiality was rare. During the final game Yarmouth coach Grimshaw twice refused the Kiwanis the customary courtesy of substitute runners, usually granted when an opposition batter had been hit with a pitch. Affronted, Kiwanis players assailed Grimshaw throughout the game.

After the series Grimshaw would respond.

"There is no doubt that St. Stephen got the breaks," he told the Halifax press. "We lost two games we should have won. The earned runs will show that....

"And another thing, St. Stephen may have the Maritime Championship, but the Gateways had to show them how to lay out a diamond. They did not even have a batter's box when we went up there for the beginning of the series.... The home plate was also plenty out at the St. Stephen diamond.

"There is another thing which should not be forgotten. St. Stephen has only to defeat one team [they actually had to beat two] to enter in the Maritime Championships, but we have to go to earn the Nova Scotia title with plenty of playing, not that we are crabbin'....

"Out of Yarmouth, there will never come any crabbin'."

◆ 1 9 3 5 ◆
THE BREAK

"Do you know how many times I played that game over?"
—Orville Mitchell—

WHITNEY STREET was a dank dead end on the American side where the only treasures were desperate young women in the uniform of sin. Large cars with out-of-state plates hugged the curbs of Whitney Street—500 feet from the border—awaiting a treasure in a short, beaded skirt and inch-thick rouge to bound from the run-down, rented houses and snuggle closely. Other times, the women would come out and walk slowly around a bandstand as young men winked and flirted and ogled and beseeched a gust of wind to do something educational with those skirts.

Two regular spectators at the bandstand also pitched baseball in St. Stephen. They would sit and chat with the girls—it was usually the same pallid girls on parade—and everything was chummy until one of the pitchers came down with venereal disease. They found other places to go after that. But the girls still drifted around the bandstand, and other boys came to wink.

Decent folks prayed for these wayward, garish women of lost faith and recondite acts. Yet Whitney Street was forever a dead end for the women, whose fathers were often drunk and whose mothers could work miracles with a can of baked beans and a loaf of bread. They were survivors, not miscreants; victims, not criminals.

The border did have crimes, though. Theft primarily. Of chickens principally. In mid-decade, in fact, there was unprecedented foul filching until St. Stephen police charged two men. Each was sentenced to a year in jail. "The ring [is] believed broken," announced the press.

Town by-laws were tricky for some. Seto On, the owner of the Sanitary Cafe, was charged with keeping his establishment open past 11 p.m. on a Sunday. The overhead and taxes were too high, complained the owner. The court fined him $20. Shortly thereafter, the cafe was destroyed by fire.

By today's standards, the courts were stern and often pious. "An unusually large number of disagreeable cases were before the court," began a report in the *Saint Croix Courier*, adding that one case concerned the corruption of a 15-year-old girl whose letters were so vile that "[the judge] ordered the court constable to burn them at once."

Violent crime was rare. When a local man, upon entering his vestibule, was cracked on the forehead and robbed of $700, the Royal Canadian Mounted Police made an immediate assumption: "Knowing the character of the residents of the County ... such a brutal crime must be the work of outsiders." It seems outsiders as often as not meant trouble. They rolled into town seeking fun or profit, and found both in bootlegged booze craved by Americans living under the scourge of the 18th Amendment.

The amendment, or the National Prohibition Act, would ban the manufacture, sale and possession of liquor from 1920 to 1933. During that time, the Canadian border crossings at St. Stephen, Calais and the two Milltowns were hubs of booze smuggling. (Temperance acts varied from province to province. By the late 1920s, however, most provinces had voted "wet," and New Brunswick did so in 1927.)

At one St. Stephen-area crossing, a Montreal-based duo transported booze in a modified auto trimmed with copper tubing that ran through the roof, down the sides, around the back and beneath the car. The tubing was filled through a hole in the roof and held 100 gallons of 30-proof. It worked well until an alert customs officer asked the right question at the wrong moment, sending the couriers fleeing on foot. Most wise booze smugglers, however, "ran the port" in the wee hours past snoozing customs officers. Without a border patrol to give chase, culprits were home free. Still, booze was the target of "one of the greatest drives on lawbreakers ever made on the border" when early in the decade an undercover cop posed as "a big potato from Aroostock"—a small New Brunswick town approximately 150 miles north of St. Stephen—and helped arrest seven bootleggers in Milltown, New Brunswick, said the *Courier*. The minimum fine for a first offence was $500 or six months in jail.

St. Stephen was overseen by a leaden sheriff's department long the domain of Sheriff R. A. Stuart, who retired in 1932 at age 90. At mid-decade, the most active law-enforcement agency in town was a three-man police force that included, for a time, Ernest Woodard. A former toolmaker, Night Officer Woodard was a squat, broad-shouldered man in his late 30s who was diligent in his role as upholder of public order.

"He was after everybody and he wanted to arrest everybody," remembers Roy Boles, himself a policeman for more than a quarter of a century. "He had this uniform on, and it never fit him very good: it was a little too big; the legs came down a little too far; but then, sometimes, they were a little too high. And he always had this bulge there under his tunic. Maybe he had a gun, or maybe that's where he kept his billy club, or maybe it was handcuffs—I don't know."

Woodard served from 1933 to 1937, during which time he was kicked, punched, cussed, beaten with sticks and assaulted with a large flashlight. One day in 1935 Night Officer Woodard—working 84 hours a week and earning $90 a month—asked the town fathers for a raise. The councillors promptly placed the request on their agenda, debated it and turned it down.

Two years later, Night Officer Woodard, generally praised for his courage, honor and two-fisted approach to justice, resigned from the force and joined the federal customs department as a seasonal fireman. ◆ ◆ ◆ ◆

The Dow Brewery team from Montreal was "a bunch of amateurs rated about the best in their class in Canada," proclaimed the *Saint Croix Courier* in 1936. In truth, many were highly skilled players from American and Canadian colleges who had been fortunate enough to land these wonderful summer jobs. They travelled in their own railway car and sported gleaming red-and-white uniforms. "We'd never seen anything like that," gushed one Maritime opponent. "God those uniforms were beautiful, just beautiful."

Dow Brewery came that summer to the St. Croix Valley to play the Southerners, a senior-level team from Calais that had recently been tromped 16-6 by the Kiwanis. Despite Kiwanis' efforts to arrange what would probably have been billed as an Eastern Canada showdown, the Montreal team beat the Calais team 9-2, then left the area immediately. The town of St. Stephen was not amused.

"[Montreal's pitcher] the celebrated LaHale ... or one of his mates, was using emery dust, or some other material to roughen the surface of the balls, another feature that left a bad taste in the mouths of real fans," raged the *Courier*. "Five balls were thrown out of the game and [Calais pitcher Ken] Kallenberg's index and second fingers were raw on the tips where the scarifying substance had scraped the skin. The club had been unbeaten before Monday on their tour and with good reason if it was allowed to get away with such tactics everywhere. Nothing was left to chance. There was even an umpire along to run the game."

A few days later, as the Montreal team was preparing to leave the Maritimes, its manager told a Halifax newspaperman in Yarmouth that the Gateways were the best team they had played in two years. The *Courier* scoffed. "Remembering what the Kiwanis have done with Yarmouth and other Nova Scotia champions the last four years," the newspaper concluded, "nothing more need be said."

As the Dow Brewery players returned home in their private railway car, the Kiwanis continued to talk of a match in Montreal that year. The talk proved fruitless, however.

No Maritime senior baseball club travelled in the style of the Dow Brewery team. Indeed, in 1935 just motoring from town to town on Maritime roads meant misadventure for ballplayers.

"In the early days," recalls Orville Mitchell, "we didn't have that much money and we had to hire taxis to go to Moncton. We'd put our ball uniforms on in St. Stephen and drive in those open cars clean to Moncton, and get there at 12 o'clock and get something to eat in the restaurant and go right to the baseball diamond tireder than hell, riding five or six hours on the gravel road.

"I went to Saint John and it was just mud, and the alders used to be hittin' the cars. It used to take us five hours to get to Saint John— it was 90 miles then. About every 15 miles we'd have a flat tire, get out, get the jack, take the tire off, take the tube out, patch it, get the tube in, put the tire back on the wheel, take the hand pump, and pump 'er up and away you'd go. Then another 15 or 20 miles you'd have another flat. We'd get there and play a double-header and leave the city about 10 o'clock, after we had somethin' to eat. And it would be two or three or four o'clock in the morning by the time we got home. And foggy! It was so foggy, you couldn't go over 10 miles an hour. You couldn't see. One night we started for home and got as far as West Saint John and turned around and had to stay in a hotel."

Humor helped pass the time along the way. Squirrelly Ross was the centre of attention during one ride to Newcastle. Outfielder George Purcell, who drove a taxi at the time, was giving the team a lift when Ross asked nervously about the speed.

Purcell pointed to a dial. "A hundred and ten," he said calmly.

"Oh cripes!" screamed Ross, who often suffered from motion sickness. "You better slow down."

It was some time before the nearly hysterical Ross could be convinced that Purcell had jokingly pointed to the radio dial.

The only successful Maritime team to have its own vehicle was the Yarmouth Gateways. Dubbed a "bus" because more suitable terms were either impolite or not invented, the vehicle was compliments of H. H. Raymond, president of Eastern Steamship Lines. Raymond summered outside Yarmouth, and for a period the bus transported his guests from the airport to his estate. It was transportation unlike anything previously experienced by the visiting New York elite. An old Hudson automobile constituted the front of the bus, and at the back was a fragile, make-shift trailer. Half a dozen windows ran down either side. It sat 10 comfortably.

"It was the meanest-made thing you ever saw," says Gateways pitcher Nate Bain. "That car wouldn't be allowed on the road today. There was a rumble seat in the back of the car, and that was taken out and this ball-bearing fixture was put in. In the bus there were wire struts between two pieces that were almost like cardboard. I think it was plyboard, a quarter-inch thick. The struts were the only reinforcement. The bus only had two wheels. It wasn't dual wheels, either, it was just ordinary wheels. And it had a telephone system— a speaker system, really—from the driver to the back. Most of us played penny ante at the back."

Once, on the way to Springhill on a long dirt road, driver Pete LeBlanc alighted from the bus and peered anxiously at a rear tire. It was about half deflated.

"How many of you in there?" LeBlanc asked his passengers.

"'Bout 11," came the answer.

"OK," said the driver, taking command. "I want nine of you to sit on that one side to take the weight off the tire. And I want two of you on the other side for balance."

The players complied, crunching on top of one another all the way to Springhill.

More than once, however, long-distance travel on poorly lit, haphazardly maintained roads proved nearly fatal. James Brennan, a catcher for the Springhill Fence Busters, was struck and badly injured by an on-coming car while he was inspecting his tires. Two members of the Connecticut Yankees barnstorming team were in a mishap in Truro, Nova Scotia, and Halifax teams experienced several close calls to and from ball games.

Dangers aside, the trips were chances to share the company of others on the way to defend the home town's honor. All of the better ball teams had half a dozen or so members who could harmonize during the driving hours. They would try a familiar song—anything possessing a little verse was good enough, such as Irving Berlin—and, with contributions from everyone in the car, they would remember most of the words, most of the time. Among the Kiwanis, Orville Mitchell sang bass, baritone or even a little tenor; Ike Vanstone was a tenor; Charlie Godfrey sang bass; Muddy McLain, a tenor, was the lead singer, despite a severe stutter when he spoke.

"There were a bunch of us that always travelled in the same car," says Laurie Thorborne, of the Liverpool Larrupers, a Nova Scotia powerhouse late in the decade. "Every trip you were on, there was always singin' goin' on. You didn't know what in the world was goin' by ya. One time Vic Winters, who always played the mouth organ, was drivin'. We were goin' along, and up on the side of the road there was this fella wavin' his hands and wavin' and wavin'. And, all of a sudden, the train shot across the crossing, and Vic put 'er in the ditch, and when he came out of the ditch, the last of the train had just done by. We thought we were gone."

Thorborne remembers leaving Springhill in a car with Shorty Broom, who was driving, and Nels Deveau. "So we were drivin' along and I said , 'Shorty, I hear a train.' He said, 'Can't [hear it].' The fog was so bad. Then I could hear the car bumpin' along and *feel* the car bumpin' along, and here we were goin' up along a railway track! And then I heard the train again! We all got out of the car and guided [Broom] back so he could get back on the road. Lucky we weren't too far from the crossing. We had just gotten off the track, and the train went by."

In July 1935 the *Courier* took it upon itself to solicit transportation for the Kiwanis, who were planning a five-game road trip that

August to Cape Breton Island. The payment for any takers would be $2. "That money is small inducement for a long drive that will consume three weekdays, but a good time is assured. Planning a vacation soon? Take your car and head for Sydney with a few ball players aboard."

◆　◆　◆　◆

The Cape Breton odyssey began on a Thursday in the wee hours. Late that first afternoon the Kiwanis arrived in Westville, Nova Scotia, approximately 80 miles from Cape Breton, beat the local Miners 3-1, then hopped in cars "with the dust of the Nova Scotia roads and visions of supper in their eyes," the *Courier* reported.

The team continued on after supper. "Three of the four cars in the caravan rolled onto the Cape Breton ferry landing at one o'clock in the morning," the *Courier* said. The driver of the fourth car "had read signs wrong at Antigonish, and had doubled back to New Glasgow. Near daybreak everyone got tired of throwing rocks at the fish and the party went to bed in Port Hawkesbury leaving the babes in the woods to their fate. All were back together again at breakfast and made the last leg of the trip well-bunched."

The next day, before 5,000 fans, the Kiwanis played New Waterford, leaders of the Cape Breton Colliery League and undefeated in 15 games that season. The teams battled to a 10-inning, 2-2 draw with New Waterford scoring twice in the bottom of the ninth. In Sydney the following morning, the Kiwanis defeated that city's senior entry, 4-2.

Later that bright August day, they faced the Boston Royal Colored Giants, a polished barnstorming "Negro" team and frequent opponent in St. Stephen. Sydney billed this game as the clash of titans and accorded it the appropriate pomp. "Each club lined up in front of the stands and stood with bared heads while the band played the Canadian and American anthems," reported the *Courier*. "At least it was supposed to play the Canadian national song, but after stumbling over a few notes of *O Canada* and panicking entirely on the end of the second bar, they went into a huddle and came out playing *God Save the King*. The leader had a score of *The Star Spangled Banner* evidently for the boys had no trouble with that."

Exhausted, the Kiwanis lost 11-0.

But the day was not over. The team had unwisely scheduled a third game, against the Boston Colored Giants, to be played 18

The Great Fire, St. Stephen, January 1930: $200,000 in damage, 13 businesses lost, three families left homeless. (CHARLOTTE COUNTY MUSEUM)

St. Stephen Mohawks, 1931 Maritime Senior Baseball Champions. Front row (left to right): Laurie Crompton, Ray Jellison, Harry Boles, Bill Whitlock, Arthur Middlemiss, Sheldon Laughlin (scorer), Roy Boles, George Purcell, George Lee. Back row: Howdy Clark, Raymond Moffatt, Theo McLain, Gordon Coffey, Orville Mitchell, Ike Vanstone. (N.B. SPORTS HALL OF FAME)

Downtown St. Stephen, early 1930s: A town in harmony with its appearance. (CHARLOTTE COUNTY MUSEUM)

Halley Horton, Yarmouth Gateways shortstop: The people's choice. (COURTESY HARRIET HORTON/SOUTH WEST PHOTO)

The Yarmouth Gateways' team bus: "The meanest-made thing you ever saw." (COURTESY SOUTH WEST PHOTO)

Doug Horton, Yarmouth Gateways: Slugging star and victim of the hidden-ball trick. (COURTESY HARRIET HORTON/SOUTH WEST PHOTO)

The Gateways on the Yarmouth wharf. Bottom row (left to right): Pete White, Ernie Grimshaw, George Kenney (fan), S. O'Brien (fan), the Reverend Ross (fan). Middle row: H. Lewis, Murray Veno, Lightning Amirault, Vic Murphy, Danny Landry, Jimmy Amiro, Cliffie Surette, Biss Boyd, Ron Sholds, S. Fraser. Top row: Halley Horton, Nate Bain, Red Goudey, Doug Horton. (COURTESY SOUTH WEST PHOTO)

◆St. Stephen Kiwanis, 1935: Transition from power to pitching.
(N.B. SPORTS HALL OF FAME)

◆Springhill Fence Busters, 1936 Maritime finalists. Front row (left to right): Donald Condy, Art Bonnyman, Charlie Crawford (mascot), Dannie Beaton, Artie Crawford. Middle row: Eddie Emberly, Jack Merritt, Purney Fuller, Midge Brown, Lawson Fowler. Back row: Stu McLeod, Frank Bell, Tommy Linkletter, Art Canning, Jack Fraser, Charlie Burton, Henry Dykins. Missing: Leo MacDonald. (SPRINGHILL FOTO AND GALLERY)

◆ Jack Fraser, Springhill Fence Busters: Youth and talent at second base. (NOVA SCOTIA SPORT HERITAGE CENTRE)

◆ Lawson Fowler: The heart of the Million-Dollar Infield. (COURTESY LAWSON FOWLER)

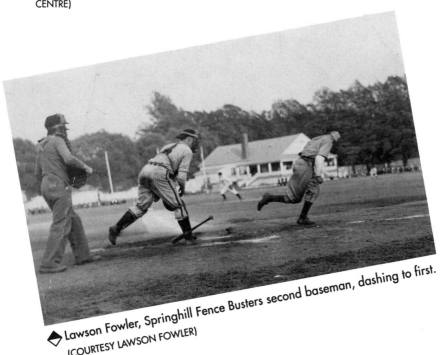

◆ Lawson Fowler, Springhill Fence Busters second baseman, dashing to first. (COURTESY LAWSON FOWLER)

◆ Babe Ruth visits the Maritimes: Desperate salutes to a baseball legend. (NOVA SCOTIA SPORT HERITAGE CENTRE)

◆ Catcher Burlin White, Boston Royal Colored Giants: Wonderful baseball skills and the smile of a great PR man. (COURTESY LAWSON FOWLER)

Tenacious Baldy Moffatt (right) and his battery, 1938 (left to right): Jim Morell, Lefty Brownell, and Charlie Godfrey. (COURTESY JIM MORELL)

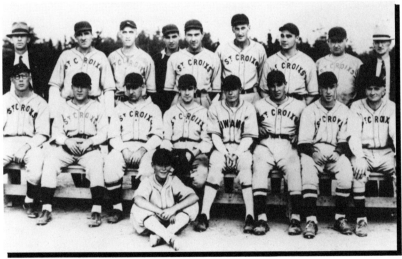

St. Stephen St. Croixs, 1938 Maritime Senior Baseball Champions. Forefront: Billy Algar (bat boy). Front row (left to right): Lefty Brownell, Dana Miles, Art Lowe, Phil McCarroll, Cliff Middlemiss, Charlie Weatherby, Don Norton, Baldy Moffatt. Back row: Arlo Hayman, Harry Boles, Rainnie Moffatt, Lloyd Kelly, Gordon Coffey, Jim Morell, Ken Kallenberg, Charlie Godfrey, Len Webber. (N.B. SPORTS HALL OF FAME)

Lefty Brownell, St. Stephen St. Croixs: "The best there was in the Maritimes." (COURTESY LEFTY BROWNELL)

Ken Kallenberg, St. Stephen St. Croixs: Pro prodigy in the uniform of the New York Giants' Carl Hubbell. (COURTESY KEN KALLENBERG/ NEW YORK GIANTS)

Liverpool Larrupers, 1939 Maritime Senior Baseball Champions. Front row (left to right): Laurie Thorborne, Carly Waters, Art Killam, Kal Seaman, Garneau Seaman, Gordon Hirtle, Fred Kenny, Danny Seaman. Back row: Raw Murray, Lloyd Young, Vic Winter, Nels Deveau, Clayton Hutchins, Ike Seaman, Burton Young, Warren Keay. (NOVA SCOTIA SPORT HERITAGE CENTRE)

miles down the road in Sydney Mines. By this point St. Stephen's pitchers were near collapse, second baseman Bill McIntosh could not move his shoulder, and the rest of the team "was tired and sick of baseball." Coach Orville Mitchell consented to play only after Burlin White, genial manager of the Colored Giants, loaned the Kiwanis one of his pitchers.

Nevertheless, fatigue would be the least of the Kiwanis' problems. On the way to the game a car carrying several players was "clipped by a big Packard. Nearly all the regulars were bunged up in the crash and it was a motley aggregation that took the field that evening," said the *Courier.*

The Colored Giants won 7-3. From all accounts, few Kiwanis cared.

In less than four days the Kiwanis had travelled 1,100 miles over frightful roads and had played five ball games—every one of them against sound opposition with something to prove. Complained young pitcher Ken Kallenberg, a Calais resident added to the Kiwanis roster for the trip: "Even my fingers are tired."

◆ ◆ ◆ ◆

At mid-decade, baseball remained part of the bordertown psyche amid tragedies big and small. A woman carrying a dish filled with gas had flames ignite and blow into her face; a two-year-old's arm was caught up to the elbow in the wringer of an electric washer; and the chief electrician at Canadian Cottons in Milltown, New Brunswick, was hit by 6,900 volts while fixing a transformer.

Kiwanis right fielder Earl (Squirrelly)Ross was not having great luck, either. "A series of tough breaks, beginning with a serious illness and operation for Mrs. Ross the previous winter, and a fire at his house a few weeks ago, have put Squirrelly on his back," reported the *Courier.* But Mrs. Ross recovered quickly, the house was repaired, and soon Earl was Squirrelly once more, seemingly living under his very own full moon.

Squirrelly had started chewing tobacco at age 10 and, according to an old pal, had stopped growing around that age, too. Nicknamed Squirrelly for his quick, jerky movements or for stuffing the tails of dead squirrels into his cap when he was a boy, Ross had little formal education. "How much more than 1.000 can I hit?" he once earnestly asked a teammate. The teammate laughed, so, as usual, Ross laughed, too. Happiness, not arithmetic, was the essence of the lad who began working in the cotton mill in his teens and was still actively employed in a factory as he approached age 90.

Still, Ross was sensitive.

"He once tried to steal a base on his own without a signal from me," recalls playing coach Mitchell. "I balled him out and I almost broke his heart. He almost cried ... He wouldn't pay attention. You'd give him a signal, and he didn't know what a signal was half the time. To make the hit and run effective, he's got to be stealing and take the second baseman with him. If he didn't, [the batter] is left high and dry. I'd put on a hit-and-run sign, and the next thing you knew he was still standin' there."

"Squirrelly always wanted to steal third base," continues Gordon Coffey. "And he'd always get thrown out. And the coach would give him hell. Then he'd come to the bench and we'd all give him hell. And Squirrelly wouldn't say a word until everything was quieted down. And then you'd hear him, 'By Jesus, I'll make it the next time.'"

On the road, Ross was a practical joker, his antics becoming part of the lore in each community he visited. In Yarmouth, for example, he poured a bedpan full of urine and butted cigarettes down on teammates sneaking up the fire escape.

"Once, we were on the road and we were havin' dinner on the ferry," recalls Mitchell. "Squirrelly was sittin' at the table and was just about to get up, and we looked and he had cleaned all the table of silverware. He had it all stuffed in his pocket. I had to take it all out. I said, 'Christ, you'll get us all arrested.'"

Ross attempted to steal silverware again, on the Digby ferry en route to Yarmouth, and veteran outfielder George Purcell recalls his teammates turning Ross upside down and shaking the goods out of him.

"If you were in a hotel and were takin' a shower and you came out with a nice big towel, he'd be there sayin', 'Now, isn't that dandy.' You'd have to tell him to wait, that he could have it first thing in the morning," Purcell says.

Pitcher Kallenberg recalls the time a "half-looped" Orville Mitchell fell down a long flight of stairs in a Saint John hotel. "He comes out there and steps right off and misses every damn step and lands right on the floor. He must've come down 14, 18 steps. Squirrelly Ross is at the bottom, and he yells, 'Safe !'"

One time in Woodstock, New Brunswick, during a rare appearance as a catcher, Ross watched as the home side knocked around the Nothin' Ball of his pal, Howdy Clark. "Squirrelly didn't wear a breast protector, and if there were men on base, he didn't wear a mask," says Gordon Coffey. "He would say, 'I can't see to throw.' Well, along in this game, Woodstock had a man on third base. Then this fella hit a little Texas leaguer out in left field, and the runner looked at it and was pretty sure of himself, and started for home. And then, all of a sudden, Squirrelly runs out and says, 'Nice catch,' and he's pounding in his glove. The runner sees this and goes back to third. The thing is, the outfielder didn't catch the ball at all! Squirrelly fooled him. Of course, he and Howdy had had a couple of beer before the game...."

As a ballplayer, Ross was tenacious, having the ability to "look at the sun and see right through it," according to fellow outfielder Coffey. He used above-average speed to snare balls other outfielders conceded as hits. Shortstop Phil McCarroll, who joined the team in mid-decade, says other players received applause after making a nice catch; the fans gave Ross their change.

Ross was a stubborn hitter with quick wrists and extraordinary vision. "I could see the stitches when the ball left [the pitcher's] hand," he brags. His combination of skills resulted in absurd sessions of consecutive foul balls. "Against Charlie Nichols [a Minto, New Brunswick, native who tried out with the Cincinnati Reds] I hit 18 foul balls, one right after another, and lost them all, I think. I wanted to hit the ball, but it was those god-damned knuckle balls he was firin': I could see them comin' home, but I couldn't get a good whack at them. That's all the balls they had, 18. And I kept sayin' to him, 'Throw me a good one.' When he did, I got a three-bagger."

Against the Boston Braves in 1934, Ross had two hits in three at-bats, and scored one of his team's three runs. The *Courier* called him "a tower of strength."

Ross liked that.

During that memorable contest Ross had one of his foul ball episodes, causing Braves manager Bill McKecknie to complain: "Look at that little son of a bitch out there workin' the ass off the best pitcher I got."

Ross liked that, too.

◆ ◆ ◆ ◆

The Kiwanis opened the New Brunswick semi-finals with a 5-4 loss to Devon, champions of the York-Sunbury League. There were 15 errors, eight by Devon, seven by St. Stephen. The Kiwanis won the second game 15-6, setting up a deciding game in St. Stephen. Lefty Brownell got the call for the Kiwanis.

Cecil (Lefty) Brownell was actually born *right-handed*. As an infant, he fell into a scalding wash tub, and his right hand contracted slightly inward. After the hand had healed, a window came crashing down "and busted it up again." So Brownell became a Lefty.

"In Grade One the teacher tried to make me use the right hand," he says, "but I wouldn't. They used to strap the hand behind my back when I used to go in and sit down. They used to put the pencil in my right hand, but I was stubborn and I wouldn't use it. I developed left-handed."

His hands were small for a pitcher, but powerful; his muscular shoulders sloped, giving his torso a triangular look; and his head was always tilted at an angle. At five-foot-eight and 170 pounds, Brownell seemed a larger man. He never moved too quickly, and he spoke with a drawl. A small pair of specs resting on the bridge of his nose made Brownell look a tad like a working man's professor. His favorite pitching apparel, even in temperatures of 90° Fahrenheit, was long wool underwear and a long-sleeved shirt. After games he would wring out the sweat.

Fellow pitcher Ken Kallenberg calls Brownell aloof. "You take a bunch of guys, and all together they can laugh about certain things. Lefty was more or less sitting on the outside, listening, above it all … but he was a helluva nice guy, too.… Most left-handers are a little strange, anyway."

At age 14, he had pitched scrub games on small fields in West Saint John, where he was noticed by one of the city's five senior teams, St. Rose. When asked to pitch for St. Rose, Brownell declined. Days later, team managers were knocking on Brownell's door.

"You know what's wrong with you?" said one of the men, stabbing his finger in Brownell's face. "You're yellow! You got a big yellow streak up and down your back!"

Less than a week later Brownell was into his first wind-up for St. Rose and staring in at his first hitter, Charlie Gorman, the world's fastest skater and Saint John's most truculent ballplayer.

"He was a left-handed batter, and my very first pitch I threw him a drop curve," Brownell recalls. "Now, I always threw right at the batter, and the ball would break away from them. But this one didn't—it hit him right in the back. He turned around and hauled his hat off and pounded it on the home plate and jumped on it. Then he looked at me and grabbed the bat and took three or four steps towards me, and stopped. I was just a kid. I was looking for some place to run."

He lasted only three innings that day for St. Rose, but Brownell would have other days.

The first time his grandmother saw him pitch, she sat for five innings and watched batter after batter swing haplessly at his fastball and curves. Despite this overpowering performance by her grandson, the elderly woman grew despondent.

"Where's Cecil?" she eventually asked.

"That's him out there on the pitcher's mound throwing the ball," Brownell's wife explained.

"Oh my!" the grandmother moaned. "That poor boy's been out there all this time trying to hit that stick, and he hasn't hit it yet."

Brownell eventually joined another Saint John senior team, St. Peter's, but departed for St. Stephen in the winter of 1933 when the Kiwanis found him masonry work on the border.

In Saint John in June 1934, Brownell faced his old teammates for the first time. As fans taunted, "Hey, ol' sawdust arm," he stood on the mound and pledged quietly to himself that in a St. Stephen uniform he would never lose to a Saint John team. He never did.

"Brownell was just a raw pitcher," says Orville Mitchell, Brownell's first coach in St. Stephen. "He never learned to pitch until he came to us, and you'd almost have to drive it into his head because he was as stubborn as old hell. And he'd get excitable, too. I don't know how many times I went out to the mound to talk to him, just to calm him down."

Teammate Jim Morell remembers Brownell as always having money and a good job, this at a time when others were content to have 75 cents in their pockets. That kept Brownell independent, says Morell, a description echoed by catcher Lloyd Kelly.

"Morell and Kallenberg and I were all good friends," says Kelly, who joined the team in 1938. "Not so with Lefty. He was down to business all the time. And he was tough to catch. He had a wide curve ball [but] all you had to know is when he was going to throw that fastball. His curve ball was good, but when he threw that high, hard one, that's the one you had to be on your toes for. And you had to keep in mind that if you blew one, he was on your back in good style."

Whatever his mercurial temperament, Brownell's arrival in 1934 was timed perfectly, coming as it did when several original St. Stephen pitchers were retiring or moving on. He shared pitching duties first with stalwart Roy Boles and big Mike Calder, then with Kallenberg and Morell. More than the others, however, opponents feared Brownell. His pitches snapped, and by mid-decade, Brownell knew when and how to use a change of pace. He would vary his delivery—sidearm one pitch, three-quarters another, overhand another. His control was just imperfect enough to be an asset. "He was overpowering," says Armond Wigglesworth, a journalist from Liverpool, Nova Scotia. "If pitchers had a curve and a fastball and were left-handed, what else did they need? You can imagine left-handed hitters trying to hit him."

"He was most effective when he was wild," says coach Mitchell. "The Boston Colored Giants didn't dare stand in there and get a foothold. He didn't do it intentionally—he was wild. And the wilder he was, the better he was against the colored fellas. They'd be swinging at balls in self-defence. He'd scare the hell out of them."

"I think he was a smart pitcher," says Lloyd Young, of the Liverpool Larrupers. "If you hit one of his pitches real good, you'd never see that pitch again. He'd throw everything else but that one pitch."

Says Morell, "He was like Gretzky, a winner. He was the best there was in the Maritimes. There is no doubt about that."

The deciding game of the New Brunswick semi-finals against Devon drew more than 2,000 fans to the St. Stephen diamond to witness Brownell face Dinny Dinsmore, an able and experienced right-hander. St. Stephen trailed going into the bottom of the ninth, and first up was Brownell, a mediocre hitter. Mitchell quickly searched his reserves for a pinch hitter—Roy Boles had already been used—and found none.

"OK, Lefty," Mitchell said, giving him a slight tap on the shoulder, "do the best you can."

Brownell walked to home plate and looked towards the mound.

Dinsmore's first strike buzzed past Brownell, who barely moved. The crowd's spirits sank. Brownell lunged at and missed the next pitch for strike two, then stepped out of the batter's box. Finally, he stepped back in. Dinsmore delivered.

"He threw one breaking away from me, and I teed off on 'er," recalls Brownell. "The centre fielder came runnin' over, and the ball started curvin'. He didn't get to it. It landed on the race track and went into the bushes. I headed for first, then second, and when I came around third, they were hootin' and hollerin' and wavin' me in and everything else. I was just a steam engine after pitchin' the game, huffin' and puffin'. Finally, I started for home plate. I think for three minutes I didn't touch ground again. All the players were there throwin' me in the air. That was the first, last and only home run I ever hit.

"When I hit that home run, Dippy Burns—he was the iceman at that time and used to deliver big chunks of ice—was in the grandstand. He got a big, soft hat and jumped up and turned it over and went right along the grandstand holding out the hat. And they were throwing in dollar bills and change. When he got done he folded up the hat and brought it down to me. There was a little under $100 in there."

The run tied the game and pushed it into extra innings. In the bottom of the 12th with two out and the bases empty, Gordon Coffey singled, then stole second base. Muddy McLain singled, scoring Coffey with the series-winning run.

The Kiwanis' victory appeared fleeting, however, when the president of the New Brunswick Amateur Baseball Association, St. Stephen's Bill Whitlock, immediately ordered the game replayed. Kiwanis outfielder Art Lowe had not been officially registered to play, Whitlock said. In the replay a few days later, Brownell again beat Dinsmore, this time 7-3.

After the game Dinny Dinsmore, twice beaten in critical games, wept.

St. Stephen went on to sweep the Saint John Trumps in three games to win their fifth consecutive New Brunswick senior baseball championship. Not only did the Trumps lose the series, but they failed behind the scenes as well.

The Trumps' owner, a man named Stevens, who also ran the Stevens Construction Company in Saint John, was $3,000 or $4,000 in the red with his ball team, says Kiwanis coach Orville

Mitchell. Mitchell remembers Stevens pulling him aside at a function. "He said, 'Look, you're two games up on us. If I can just get two home games, I can get some of my money back. I'll make it worth your while if you pitch anybody but Brownell against us in St. Stephen.' I said, 'I'll think it over, and you'll know my decision when the battery is announced.' There he was at the third game on the bench, and our scorekeeper goes over and announced the battery—Brownell and [McLain]. Jesus Christ, he called me everything but a white man." ◆ ◆ ◆ ◆

In the 1935 Nova Scotia finals, the Yarmouth Gateways blasted the Cape Breton champions, the Dominion Hawks, in three straight games to take the provincial title. The series included a 14-0 embarrassment in game one, in which Gateways' slugger Doug Horton clouted a home run into East Indian Bay. ("Someone went out and got the ball," says Horton, "and it was just drippin'.")

Not surprising then, heading into the Maritime championship series, wagering in Yarmouth favored the local boys over the Kiwanis two to one.

Game one matched the Maritimes' top pitchers, Copie LeBlanc and Lefty Brownell, and their performances validated the billing. The score was 1-1 after seven innings, and 2-2 after eight. Into extra innings they battled, neither pitcher weakening and neither team bending. In the bottom of the 11th with one out, Doug Horton doubled to left, bringing LeBlanc to the plate.

"It was a perfect setting for Copie," reported H. J. Osborne in the Saint John *Telegraph-Journal*, "as he strode to the plate with his big willow ... here was his chance of evening at least one of those lost games of previous years. He banged a hit into centre sending Horton home with the run that won."

It was St. Stephen's first extra-inning loss in either a New Brunswick or a Maritime final. Typical of their 1935 season, they committed four errors and seemed to be running on empty. Veterans such as second baseman and coach Orville Mitchell and infielder Bill McIntosh strained with diminished skills, while injuries drained catcher Muddy McLain and outfielder George Purcell. Roy Boles was having a poor year, and Lefty Brownell was overworked. The Gateways' indefatigable player-coach Ernie Grimshaw sensed the kill.

At a banquet between games someone suggested to Grimshaw

that the Kiwanis were still confident. Grimshaw smirked and sniffed, "Good luck to them."

But luck was scarce for St. Stephen. Aided by four more Kiwanis errors, Yarmouth won game two 6-2, taking a two-game lead in the series. "The Kiwanis today displayed their poorest form since they were crowned tri-province champions in 1931," Osborne wrote in the *Telegraph-Journal.*

Many saw the dethroning as imminent, among them Halifax columnist Ace Foley, who referred to the Kiwanis as "fading titleholders" and noted that "supporters of the champions [could] read the handwriting on the wall".

Despite the deficit and the predictions, the Kiwanis arrived home to "a reception as hearty as the team has ever received on returning victorious,." reported the press. They also received some unexpected moral support. "Bury the hatchet," read a telegram from the Devon players, whom the Kiwanis had beaten in the New Brunswick semi-final. "We are with you to a man. Come through."

Throughout the Maritimes people followed the series passionately. The usual inning-by-inning accounts appeared in the office windows of the *Courier.* In Saint John, radio station CHSJ interrupted regular programming to announce the result of each half-inning, and a special telephone line at the *Telegraph-Journal* announced the score.

September 22, the date of game three, dawned adversely for the champions. Brownell—an essential player to any comeback hopes—lay weak and in bed with the flu. There appeared little chance that he would play in the rest of the series, let alone that day. But around noon he pulled on his long underwear and headed for the ball diamond.

Three hours later, he crawled back into bed—a winner. He had held Yarmouth to five hits, while the Kiwanis had preyed upon left-hander Cliffie Surrette. The score was 6-2.

Starters Roy Boles and Copie LeBlanc dominated game four. Boles, using the skills that had made him, for a time, the region's premier playoff pitcher, worked smoothly and effortlessly in what the *Courier* would call "one of the most brilliant performances of his whole career."

With St. Stephen leading 1-0 going into the ninth, Gateway outfielders Lightning Amirault and Nate Bain both singled. With men on first and second and no outs, Mitchell made one of his most discussed coaching decisions: he removed Boles even though his veteran pitcher was still working on a shutout.

"I had Brownell warming up," recalls Mitchell. "This had worked out pretty good for us all through the year. Halley Horton was coming to bat [soon], a right-handed hitter, and I hesitated to put Brownell in there."

Still, Mitchell waved for Brownell. Boles, expressionless as always, received a standing ovation as he walked off. It would be Boles' last game for St. Stephen.

On one of his first pitches, Yarmouth centre fielder Red Goudey smacked the ball back to Brownell, who scooped it up. Hoping to get the swift Amirault, Brownell threw to third baseman Harry Boles. Making one of his rare mistakes, Harry stepped off the bag prematurely. Amirault was safe, the bases were loaded.

Halley Horton, Nova Scotia's most popular and possibly best player, now stood at home plate, bringing about the scenario Mitchell had anticipated.

"I thought if Brownell with that fastball could get it low and to the inside, that Horton would hit a ground ball, and we'd have a force out and maybe even a double play at the plate," explains Mitchell.

The plan failed. "Brownell threw the damn ball in there just about letter-high and on the inside, and [Horton] hits it out over shortstop."

Recalls Horton: "I remember Charlie Godfrey said to me before the third game, 'You sure like those hooks, don't ya.' So the next day, when I came up with three on, I said to myself that I was not going to see any hooks. The count was two-and-two, and everything was fast, straight balls. Then he gave me a high one. I saw that ball go out and I saw [centre fielder] Coffey turn tail and run. There were three men ahead of me, and I didn't want to run anybody down. I jogged."

Amirault, Bain and Goudey all scored, and Horton stood on second. That one swing proved to be enough. Yarmouth won 3-1, ending St. Stephen's reign as Maritime champions.

(After the final out, the usually frosty LeBlanc tossed his glove aloft. "The fans who watched LeBlanc after the last out," pointed out the *Courier*, "saw as much a display of emotion as the phlegmatic Frenchman ever permitted himself.")

"Do you know how many times I played that game over?" asks

Mitchell. "A thousand times. Still haven't won it. I often said if I had pulled the outfielders in a little closer.... We just lost it on one stroke of the bat."

Meanwhile, the Gateways basked in their hard-earned glory. "On the way home we got to the Digby wharf and we saw this band and we didn't know what was goin' on," says Doug Horton. "The next thing we know, the mayor of Digby is out there to greet us, and they wanted us to go and have dinner with them."

All along the French Shore, between Digby and Yarmouth, fans lined the road. "We stopped the bus and talked to people. They had flags out and they were serenading us for winning the title," Doug Horton says. "In Yarmouth, if we'd have had someone out there collecting money, we could have each got enough money to build a house."

A few days later, the Gateways hosted the Boston Braves of the National League. Apart from outfielder Lightning Amirault beating Braves outfielders in a distance-throwing contest, the game was a major disappointment for Yarmouth and its newly crowned champions. The Gateways committed 12 errors and lost 20-2.

◆ 1 9 3 6 ◆
BALDY AND
THE BABE

"He doesn't fool anybody when he tries to act like a man."
—Ace Foley—

"**B**ABE RUTH was more than a man," reflected American sports columnist Jimmy Cannon in 1969. "He was a parade all by himself, a burst of dazzle and jingle, Santa Claus drinking whiskey straight and groaning with a bellyache caused by gluttony.... Babe Ruth made the music that his joyous years danced to in a continuous party."

The party on the baseball diamond ended for George Herman Ruth in 1935, after 28 games in the uniform of the Boston Braves and just days after an ostentatious farewell in which he defiantly crashed three home runs in one game.

One year later, the world was still trying to comprehend the unencumbered grandeur of the Sultan of Swat and his statistics: led or tied for the American League home run title 12 times, led the league in runs-batted-in five times, hit above .370 six times, a .690 lifetime slugging average and 714 home runs.

From the moment he joined the Boston Red Sox as a left-handed pitcher in 1914, and all though his prime years with the New York Yankees, myths and rumors swirled about this alumnus of a school for wayward boys. The son of a Baltimore saloon keeper, Ruth could consume 25 hot dogs in one sitting, then settle the glut with one monstrous belch. His appetite for philandering was equally gargantuan, a condition that marriage did little to curb.

"I took a lot of Babe's phone calls on the road and it was a most interesting chore," his second wife, Claire, wrote in her sentimental book *The Babe and I*. "He was certainly called by an awful lot of women. At first I thought they were vestiges of his gay bachelor days, and there is no reason to assume even now that a lot of them weren't exactly that."

Still, Ruth was perhaps the century's most important athlete, a man of grand deed and boyish manner who, nearly single-handedly, restored virtue to a national pastime defiled in 1919 by the "Black Sox Scandal." Ruth's fame was akin to that of American presidents George Washington and Abraham Lincoln. To foreigners, his popularity exceeded that of current President Calvin Coolidge. In that era, only the Prince of Wales was photographed more often.

Ruth spent the early part of his retirement vacationing, fronting for products he rarely used and enjoying, as always, being the Babe. Dr. G. A. L. Irwin, a native of Westville, Nova Scotia, and one of Ruth's friends in New York, finally convinced him to vacation in Nova Scotia. The Maritimes sucked in its belly and extended its hand to the might Babe.

On July 4, 1936, Ruth, his wife, Claire, and several hangers-on arrived in Yarmouth aboard the SS *Acadia*. Once on shore, he signed autographs for more than 100 children and many adults, and was only able to escape the adoring throng by tossing aloft handfuls of coins. With a loud roar of laughter, Ruth dashed off while children scrambled after the money.

From there, the press reported, he drove his "low sports model" through the Annapolis Valley, over what were likely the poorest roads he had ever traversed, to a plush suite in Halifax's Nova Scotian Hotel. Awaiting him was an interview with a cigar-chomping, fedora-wearing votary, *Halifax Chronicle* sports editor Wilfred (Ace) Foley.

"If I live to be 100 years old," Foley wrote the next day in his column, "I'll always remember my first glimpse of Babe Ruth.

"Accompanied by cameraman Bob Chambers, who has seen the Babe hit home runs in New York and elsewhere, I went to the hotel last night for pictures and a story.

"We found the room number, grabbed a cab (aw, okay, we took an elevator) and knocked on the door. As we waited patiently on the door step, not wishing to miss anything but trying not to appear too eager or too small-townish, a big guy burst out of the room, and, in a voice that threatened to raise the roof, he shouted: 'What do you guys want?'...

"He was over six feet tall, his hair was up in the air, he weighed over 200 pounds and still looked fit and attired in a sports shirt thrown open at the neck, one could see he had hair on his chest.

"He was BABE RUTH!"

In his main story on the great event, Foley wrote: "This was not the great big baseball idol, The Sultan of Swat, but just a big overgrown kid who worried because his beloved daughter and his friends were overdue.

"He was thinking of accidents and other things only a loving mother could conjure in her too-fertile mind, and when the late-comers did appear at the door the Babe bounded off the chesterfield with an awe-inspiring leap that startled everybody in the room and a roar that scared people for blocks around.

"That's a good word picture of the Babe. He's a great big guy (he looked immense as he lumbered through the hotel door to answer our knock) with a voice that rumbled and shakes pictures on the wall.

"He had a big shaggy head, there is hair on his chest and he looks the part he has played in life—a big he-man who hit home runs as nobody has ever done before or since and a fellow who would be good to his mother....

"He's just a great big kid at heart, and he doesn't fool anybody when he tries to act like a man."

Then came the stale questions and the mechanical answers, the ones heard every time Ruth granted an interview outside of New York City. Yet in places such as Halifax, Nova Scotia, to reporters such as Ace Foley and to thousands of Maritime readers vicariously sitting next to Ruth on that sofa, it all mattered—every syllable, pause, utterance and gesture.

How's your golf game, Babe?

"I play a good game, 73, 74 and 75 on the best courses."

What about Boston's collapse in the American League?

"I've been puzzlin' over that for some time now."

What about the Yankees?

"This kid hitter, DiMaggio, from what I've seen of him, is a great help to the team."

What was your greatest thrill?

"The day I pointed to a flagstaff in deep right field in Chicago in the World Series of a few years back, laughed into the faces of the Chicago fans and then hit the ball right where I pointed. Boy, that was a sock!"

And your next greatest thrill?

"The day last year in Pittsburgh when I hit those three home runs. Boy, did those balls go far."

In the afterglow of the most important interview of his career, Foley observed that Ruth "knows how to talk to newspaper men. When he's asked a question he doesn't care to answer he doesn't answer."

Half a century later, Foley claims he and Ruth had an understanding. "He knew I was an old-fashioned reporter and that, if he was kidding, I wouldn't quote him."

The press carried daily stories of Ruth's visit. Many had accompanying photographs, rare for local coverage of the day: Ruth catching Nova Scotia salmon in St. Mary's River near Stellarton; Ruth splitting some wood; Ruth blistering his feet while fishing; Ruth wearing a Glengarry tartan in Pictou posing with his wife and daughter; and Ruth feasting on lobster.

On the Ashburn golf course in Halifax, he played 18 holes and scored a remarkable 76, and Alex Nickerson, the young sports editor of the *Halifax Herald*, noted each twitch of the perspiring deity.

"On the eighteenth hole his first drive landed in the woods to the left. 'Gimme another ball,' he roared in a fog-horn voice. A small caddie came running, and tossed the ball. The Babe deftly caught it in his left hand, placed it carefully on the wooded tee and waggled his club experimentally....

"The gleaming white pellet whistled through the tall birches to the right, ricocheted off the limbs and flopped dismally to the ground.

"'Never mind it,' he shouted to the caddie, 'I'll play the first one.'

"In the clubhouse after the game, the Babe autographed dozens of score cards for the caddies. There seemed to be no end to the number of cards pressed eagerly towards him. Perspiring freely after the exertion of playing in the hot sun, the Babe looked for a minute. 'Ha, doubling up on me, eh boys? C'mon then gimme 'em fast,' he grinned as he roared at his abashed juvenile admirers."

The apex of Ruth's visit happened in the mining town of Westville on the overcast afternoon of July 7. Ostensibly, it was an exhibition game between the Westville Miners and the Liverpool Larrupers. But the game ceased in the middle of the first inning as a fanfare of car horns trumpeted the entrance of Babe Ruth. He had promised Westville management that he would drop by and hit a few balls for the fans, and the Babe was keeping his word.

Ruth crawled out of a car and, with a legion of youngsters at his heels, ambled to the Westville dugout. He inspected the display of bats—likely the largest that a Westville team ever owned—and selected the biggest of the lot. He wiped it carefully with his handkerchief, because it had just rained, and then massaged it in his large hands. "This bat's a little short, but it'll do if I can keep it dry," he said.

Only one hurdle remained. "Nobody had thought to procure a pair of shoes for the Bambino," Nickerson said in his report the next day. "A hurried search, and Jimmie Morell, Westville's six-foot imported hurler, was speedily relieved of his footwear. Ruth deftly laced his shoes, noting that the toe plate was on the wrong foot for him."

"They weren't the best shoes in the world," concedes Morell today. "They were half worn out, but they were better than no spikes at all, and he couldn't bat in the fancy shoes he had on. I think I bought them at Eaton's for $2.75, but they were all I could afford. He gave them back to me after he was done with them."

In the dugout Ruth signed more than two dozen baseballs before it was time to get down to business. Eyeing the field, he stood on the dugout steps and admonished the Westville manager, "You gotta give me some good balls."

Members of the Westville team sprinted out onto the field and took their positions, while Ruth, not having swung a bat in almost a year and carrying 10 to 20 extra pounds, walked to the plate to face Claude (Dingy) McLeod, an anxious right-hander suddenly balancing on the cusp of small-town immortality. This was McLeod's moment—time for his absolute best—full wind-up, the works.

Ruth let the first two pitches go by. Both were outside, and the Babe was in no shape to chase them. He sent the third pitch on a feeble arch in back of second base. It was caught easily. On the next pitch, Ruth connected cleanly, sending the ball into right field over the head of Fred Leadbetter. It was a fair effort, but not Ruthian by any means.

Embarrassed by his inability to master this strange little pitcher named Dingy, Ruth glared into the dugout and bellowed, "Where's the other bat? The one with the knob on it."

Out of the Liverpool dugout shot a massive man-child named Vic Winters, waving his favorite bat—the bat that no one except he used but soon to be the bat clasped by the world's most famous hands.

"Here, Babe! Use this!" Winters gushed, shamelessly appending, "I'm Babe Ruth, too! And I use this!"

Ruth, in no mood for benevolence, glanced at this beaming, animated courier. "That toothpick? You might be the Babe, but that toothpick I couldn't use. It's too small."

Ruth chose another bat from Westville's selection. Winters scuffed back to the dugout, his lower lip protruding.

Meanwhile, the murmurs of sympathy for Ruth that were welling up in the bleachers had wafted out to the pitcher's mound. Not wanting to ruin the exhibition, blemish the legend and anger a couple of thousand people who had come to see Ruth hit one out of sight, McLeod offered Ruth a lob. The great man did not appreciate the gesture.

"Don't slow down out there!" Ruth barked at McLeod, pointing at the fence. "I'll put it right out there."

Several attempts later, the best that Ruth could do was to elevate a couple of balls into the shallow outfield. He was now swinging from the heels—and still nothing. The ball—it must be the ball!— seemed dead.

"These balls must be made out of doughnuts," Ruth roared in frustration. The crowd laughed, but many were concerned that the red-faced, puffing legend was going to get hurt.

"McLeod goes out there with the Babe and he was gonna blow Babe's head off," says Liverpool pitcher Laurie Thorburne.

Finally, Ruth timed a pitch perfectly and sent the ball sailing over the right-field fence onto the streets of Westville. The crowd cheered wildly. Ruth smiled in relief. That was all, waved the Sultan of Swat. The exhibition was over.

He spent the next few days at the summer home of a friend, then left the Maritimes, vowing to return someday for a longer stay.

◆　◆　◆　◆

The summer of '36 provided a record-breaking heat wave that lingered benevolently over the St. Croix Valley, bountiful and contented. Twenty-five thousand people attended the 28th annual

St. Stephen exhibition—an agricultural, floricultural, horticultural and industrial fair lasting five nights and four days. It featured music by the Calais City Band, horse racing, a midway, cash door prizes, a poultry exhibition, an amateur photography display and a ball game featuring the St. Croixs and the Boston Colored Giants. Admission was 35 cents, and children got in free.

Across the river in Calais, Sampson the Wrestling Bear and Zip the Dog with the Human Brain sold out the 900-seat State Theatre. (They fight! They love! See the Terrific Fight Between Man and Bear. See the Dog Come to the Rescue!)

And John Barrymore was in town, along with Mary Astor, Boris Karloff, Claudette Colbert, Errol Flynn, Shirley Temple, James Cagney, Fred and Ginger, and Henry Fonda. Movies were magical then.

And in 1936 change cleansed the New Brunswick senior baseball champions, altering the soul of a town institution.

First came the new name, the St. Croixs, forced in part by the opposition of the Kiwanis service club to the ball games on Sundays. "Personal views may differ," reported the *Saint Croix Courier*, "but after all there is little question that opposition to the team playing on Sunday is quite general on this side of the river." The team continued to play on Sundays, albeit irregularly, and so what were first the Mohawks and then the Kiwanis became the St. Croixs in 1936. Named after the river, it would be the most enduring of the three appellations.

Next came numerous roster changes. Playing coach Orville Mitchell resigned to work more hours at Canadian Customs. Deft second baseman Bill McIntosh retired. Gone, too, was pitcher Roy Boles, fading but still capable, to play for and coach the Sydney Mines Ramblers in the semi-professional Cape Breton Colliery League. Outfielder George Purcell soon joined Boles in Sydney Mines.

Meanwhile, heart-throb infielder Pete Talbot of Woodland and pitchers Ken Kallenberg of Calais and Clem White of Saint John all came on board. Phil McCarroll, a young second-base wizard who shared the position in 1935, became a regular in 1936. Arthur Lowe, a talented, all-around young athlete, earned a spot in the outfield, while Shorty (The Frogtown Flash) Young joined as a utility outfielder.

The most significant change, however—and, by God, the one that would deliver them from this creeping apathy or else—was at coach. Here, a spindly, cigar-smoking cotton-mill worker named Aubrey (Baldy) Moffatt pushed back the parameters of probity and made winning the lone justification for playing.

"Picking Baldy to pilot the new ball club was a wise move," said the *Saint Croix Courier* late that spring. "Whatever the boys have in the way of grit and smartness he will bring to the surface. They may not beat everybody, but they'll be on their toes playing heads-up baseball every minute for the old fox."

Baldy Moffatt was not bald, and at 36, the old fox was not old. But thin, slicked-back hair, skin that stretched over a colossal nose and a chiselled chin all combined to present an ageless, even ghoulish, countenance. His deep-set eyes simultaneously laughed and dared. And his high voice—part cackle and part quack—chafed the ear. "If there was a hundred hollerin'," says pitcher Lefty Brownell, "you'd hear him."

Moffatt was the second oldest of 14 children of a Scottish carpenter. Born in Milltown, Maine, he began playing baseball at age 14. In his 20s, he was a member of the Milltown, New Brunswick, team in the semi-pro St. Croix Baseball League, an untamed association for which he was perfectly suited. Except for the 1930 season, when he patrolled the Mohawks' infield, Moffatt had never played for the St. Stephen senior team. (A younger brother, Rainnie, whose nervous energy never allowed him to remain still on a baseball diamond, joined the senior team in 1933. By 1936, when Baldy became coach, Rainnie was a star, thought by some to be the best shortstop in the Maritimes.)

"We didn't make any effort to bring Baldy back [in 1931] when we got Theo [McLain] back through immigration," says Mitchell, an original Mohawk. "We didn't want Baldy because he wasn't the right type of player. He was a dirty, mean athlete—the dirtiest athlete I ever saw.

"Baldy was smart and he had good players, but he wasn't a feller you'd give your all for because you didn't like him. He thought he could drive the fellas. He called them everything but gentlemen. He and Brownell fought all the time. Baldy intimidated his players."

Mitchell says Moffatt's style was honed in his semi-pro days. "One time, Baldy laid down a bunt and started towards first base and [catcher] Ike Vanstone went along behind him to pick up the ball. Just as Ike got his hands on the ball, Baldy threw down the bat on it. Ike just took off after him and gave him a punch in the back."

"He'd do anything to win the game, any little trick," says outfielder George Purcell. "He'd come in with his feet in the air and knock the ball out of your hands. And he was always arguing."

Opposing players detested him as he gloated in victory and taunted them with a nasty giggle when one of his many trick plays succeeded. "He tried to make them look foolish," says Lefty Brownell. "It hurt."

"He knew people didn't like him," says Mitchell. "But that didn't bother him any. He just thought it was a big joke. I've seen more guys draw up and hit him in the back. And he used to play shortstop. If you'd slide into second base, he just wouldn't lay a glove on ya, he'd punch you right in the belly."

As an umpire—he fancied himself a multi-dimensional baseball man—Moffatt blackened a 1933 exhibition game between St. Stephen and a team from Houlton, Maine. When a Houlton player stormed off the bench to question a call, Moffatt, his jaw jutting, stepped up and ripped off his iron face mask. As the player came within reach, Moffatt used the mask to strike him a vicious blow in the face. Blood gushed as the player, named Peabody, crumbled to the ground. Players on both teams watched in horror.

"The Moffatts were all fighters," says Mitchell. "If they couldn't find the opposition, they'd fight among themselves."

St. Stephen shortstop Phil McCarroll recalls a game in Milltown in 1930 when Moffatt was on one team and Moffatt's brother, Rainnie, was on the other. "One of them was playing second, and the other fella went in with his spikes. Bumped him, hit him hard. They fought right there on the Milltown diamond, fists flyin'."

Still, the Moffatt brothers seemed to co-exist peacefully most of the time, and most teammates preferred to call temperamental Rainnie—Ol' Fidgety—their friend. "Rainnie was a nice fella, altogether different from Baldy," says Kenny Kallenberg. "Baldy would cut your head off with a hatchet; Rainnie would find some other way."

Baldy's pugnacity extended beyond baseball. Once, during a basketball game, when an opponent seemed to have all avenues blocked, Moffatt drove the ball from close range into the player's face. "It flattened his nose right out," remembers Mitchell. A hockey goaltender—he was a poor skater—Moffatt used his stick as an axe and hacked unceasingly at oncoming forwards, sometimes chasing them up the ice to do so.

With belligerence, though, came brilliance. Lefty Brownell recalls that Moffatt would take over any player's position when he felt the player was not up to par. Moffatt would also handle a bat. "He'd get up there, and it would look like he was gonna swing, and, all of a sudden, he'd slap a little bit of a bunt down there and go like the blazes to first," Brownell says.

"Baldy Moffatt knew baseball," says Gordon Coffey. "I once watched the Pittsburgh Pirates practise for a month, and I didn't see them do anything that we didn't do under ol' Baldy. When he was out there, he ran the ball game. He was the coach, and what he wanted, and what he said, went."

During a game against the Boston Royal Colored Giants, the St. Croixs were behind by a run, and Coffey remembers being the first batter up in the seventh inning. Moffatt came up to him and outlined his plan: Coffey gets on first; Coffey is then bunted to second; the next batter hits; Moffatt himself then pinch-hits for the next player, getting to first and setting up the double steal, which would be executed on the following pitch.

"Well, I got on, and he *did* bunt me down to second," Coffey says. "The next fellow didn't hit. Then up came Baldy. Eventually, Baldy walked. I looked over at him, and he gave me the high sign. I said, 'Well, here it goes.' Anyway, I broke for third and I got there the same time as the ball. I slid the feet out from under the third baseman, and the ball went over him out into the outfield. And he wouldn't let me up. I was on the bottom, and I couldn't get up. But finally I did, and I slid into home plate, and the ball hit me in the back and rolled off into the sidelines. I turned around, and Baldy came stroking down the third base line. We beat them 3-2.

"Baldy had all that figured out before I went to bat."

"The idea of the game," Moffatt would say nearly half a century later, "is to know when to hit and when not to hit. I did a pretty good job. That's all I'll say."

◆　◆　◆　◆

In the spring of 1936 the new coach carefully assessed his troops. Power hitters of the early years had yielded to younger players who were weaker hitters but superior fielders and base runners. Theirs would be a team of different texture, no less diligent or successful, but a team influenced by a sort of anti-role model supplied by the coach.

Such was the case early that season when the St. Croixs played a Calais all-star team in several spirited contests, winning more than losing but often feeling victimized by poor umpiring. During one of the games Moffatt became immensely disturbed, and his mood blackened with each questionable call. Finally, Moffatt removed pitcher Ken Kallenberg, vowing that Kallenberg would never be beaten by "a blind umpire." Norman Buchanan took the mound, and outfielder Squirrelly Ross replaced Buchanan in the outfield.

"The game gave evidence of turning into a farce," reported the *Saint Croix Courier*, "and the crowd which had come to see a ball game and a pitcher's battle ... razzed the St. Croix team and coach constantly."

Plunging the game to new depths, Moffatt marched over to catcher Muddy McLain, snatched the catching equipment and shooed McLain from the field. The coach went behind the plate. He purposely missed the first pitch, and the ball came within a few inches of umpire Joe Phalan. The same thing happened on the next pitch: Moffatt made a token effort, and the umpire ducked. "It almost made me sick to my stomach just to see it," says Kallenberg.

Able to take no more, Phalan called time and ejected Moffatt. Fans promptly engulfed the coach and pitcher Ross, the latter an innocent accomplice. Police ran onto the field, intercepted the mob, ordered Moffatt to the sidelines and threatened to lay a charge. After a pause, spectators began to fight. Police moved in again. Moffatt stood off to the sidelines, grinning from ear to ear.

"After what transpired Tuesday night," said the *Courier*, "the management of the two outfits had better keep their boys apart ... until the St. Croix management have had a heart-to-heart talk with their coach on the subject of injuring the good name of their team."

Despite the pall, the St. Croixs won more than 80 percent of their exhibition games that season and drew better crowds than in previous seasons. They were granted a bye into the provincial semi-finals—largely because of their status as five-time New Brunswick champions—where they overpowered Minto. Next was the provincial final and the Saint John Maroons.

St. Stephen won the first two games of the series behind pitchers

Brownell and Kallenberg. Game three, rained out in Saint John, was moved to the border and placed in the lap of Saint John umpire Arthur Finnamore, a 53-year-old veteran of the Boer War and a former St. Stephen semi-pro. The St. Croixs fell behind early in game three, and the usually reserved St. Stephen fans began loudly protesting Finnamore's calls. Brownell offered his glasses to the umpire, who warned the frustrated pitcher. When Squirrelly Ross was called out at the plate for the last out of the game, angry spectators charged at Finnamore as he tried to reach his car.

"Most of them were merely curious or confined their feelings to shouting comments," reported the *Courier*, "but there were a few fiery spirits mixed in and the arbiter found the going so difficult that he fled back to the sanctuary of the playing field and made his way out by the rear grandstand."

After the game, won 5-3 by Saint John, a spectator wrote to the *Courier*: "Surely every fair minded fan, worthy of the designation of sportsman, signifying chivalry, fair play, and an ability to 'take it', must have been disgusted with the exhibition following Tuesday night's game with Saint John."

Disgust or not, the St. Croixs came out strongly in game four. Kallenberg threw a marvellous two-hitter, while second baseman Phil McCarroll scored twice and had two hits and nine assists (a throw contributing to an out). They crushed the Maroons 7-0 for their sixth consecutive New Brunswick senior baseball title.

The Maroons quickly protested to the provincial amateur baseball association, questioning the residential status of Americans Pete Talbot and Ken Kallenburg. The protest was withdrawn when it was learned that both had St. Stephen addresses for the summer.

◆　◆　◆　◆

The 1936 Maritime final served up the Springhill Fence Busters in a rematch of the infamous rain-protracted series three years earlier. Springhill had advanced with wins over Halifax Willow Parks, Westville Miners and Yarmouth Gateways. Usually a power-hitting team, Springhill's strength was now clearly pitching. They were led by former Gateway Purney Fuller, veterans Stu McLeod and Jack Merritt, and the Mountain Boy, Thomas Albert Linkletter.

Linkletter was a handsome, temperamental 20-year-old right-hander who strolled down from the mountainous environs of Springhill one spring and announced that he was a pitcher. No one ever doubted it.

At six-foot-one and 185 pounds, Linkletter had the perfect physique and the perfect psyche. He was positively fearless. His technique was scant, however, and he was wild. In his first year with the Busters, 1934, Linkletter's initial pitch would send most batters diving for cover. After that, few foes dared challenge Linkletter and his searing fastball.

Off the field, Linkletter enjoyed his libations, and often his behavior was as erratic as his fastball. Linkletter quarrelled frequently with manager Charlie Paul and quit several times during his career. His absences were short, his attitude unaltered. Second baseman and former pitcher Lawson Fowler once offered to help Linkletter with his delivery. "What the hell do you know?" Linkletter snapped, and turned away in a huff.

"I was around him a few times when he was talkin', I got the idea he was crazy," recalls St. Stephen's Ken Kallenberg. "It was talk about sex and women. That's the only thing that seemed to enter his mind, because every time I saw him he was talkin' to someone about it. At 19 years old, I didn't have too many experiences. He was too much for me. He seemed like a nice, pleasant guy, but he never stopped talkin'."

Nevertheless, many people made time to listen to Linkletter in spite of—or perhaps because of—the blue humor. It was expected, and it was fun just to be around him.

"He could play the harmonica like crazy," says Leo (Sailor) MacDonald, Springhill's first baseman and a good friend of Linkletter's. "He played for all the old-time dances and everything. And the harmonica, jeez, he could make one of them talk."

◆ ◆ ◆ ◆

Game one of the Maritime final in late September drew more than 1,500 spectators to the St. Stephen diamond to watch Purney Fuller and Lefty Brownell post zeros for the first three innings. In the fourth inning, centre fielder Gordon Coffey, considered by many to be the best amateur player in the Maritimes, came to bat with St. Stephen shortstop Rainnie Moffatt on first. Coffey had had five triples in eight play-off games that season, a streak that the Fence Busters either did not know about or chose to ignore. The result: Fuller served up a shoulder-high fastball down the heart of the plate and Coffey uncoiled into what the *Telegraph-Journal* would headline as "A Lusty Homer."

"Some of the old-timers back home thought that [Springhill centre fielder] Dannie Beaton should have caught that one," says Fence Buster second baseman Lawson Fowler. "I said he could have caught it if he had an airplane."

St. Stephen won 2-0.

A first attempt to play game two was rained out. Then, on the strength of Mountain Boy Linkletter's seven-hitter and on the Million Dollar Infield's four double plays, Springhill won game two 4-1 before 2,500 St. Stephen fans.

The series tied, the teams returned to Springhill for game three.

Few Springhillers had forgotten the embarrassment of 1933 and the manner in which this St. Stephen team had maimed the Buster reputation. The town was up for a rematch. As five carloads of Springhill ballplayers and managers rolled into the mining town, a fleet of cars rode out to meet them. In anticipation of large crowds a new grandstand enlarged the seating capacity from 400 to more than 1,000.

Game three, however, offered no reprisal for 1933. Behind Lefty Brownell's seven-hitter the St. Croixs crushed the Fence Busters 8-0. Coffey's run-scoring triple in the first inning was the winning hit. Sweet Pea McCarroll, whose flash and spirit endeared him to Fence Buster fans, had two hits and scored three runs. Wild all game, Fuller was the losing pitcher.

The last game of the season was a stage reserved for the talents of St. Croixs pitcher Ken Kallenberg, whose three-hitter led St. Stephen to a 5-0 triumph and to the Maritime championship. In addition, Kallenberg was tops offensively, going three-for-four and scoring a run.

"When he threw a ball," laments Springhill second baseman Lawson Fowler, "it looked like an aspirin tablet comin' in on ya."

That night to salute his triumph, Kallenberg, who at 19 was barely older than St. Croixs bat boy Billy Algar, decided some wickedness was in order. So the star and the bat boy roamed into the Springhill night to do some grown-up celebrating.

"I never had a drink in my life, until then," remembers Kallenberg, "but everybody else was havin' a few. So a guy came up to me in a taxi and wanted to know if I wanted any liquor. I asked him what he had, and he said gin. I didn't have any god-damned idea what gin was, but I bought a pint. Billy Algar wanted to know if he could have a taste of it and I gave him a taste. Then I took off someplace.

And I don't even know where the hell I went. I know that I got drunker than hell. I don't know who found me or how I got back to the hotel and to bed."

The next morning, facing a day-long journey home and with demons doing unspeakable things inside of his skull, Kallenberg pawed his way out of bed in pursuit of chocolates, feeling for unexplainable reasons that they would exorcise his agony. He rapidly devoured three or four or five or six until his stomach cried out that chocolates were absolutely not the solution.

Then, as thousands of Maritimers read in their morning newspapers about the young American prodigy named Kallenberg, this gifted innocent plodded through a spinning dawn, lowered his head, gagged and donated three or four or five or six chocolates to the sidewalks of Springhill.

SWEET PEA'S
SWEETEST SWING

"It was just one of those things that you dream about."
—Sweet Pea McCarroll—

A T 17, WALTER SARGENT and his wanderlust were mature, having been nurtured on books and sailors that told of marvellously exotic worlds beyond Sargent's native Barbados. So one day in the 1920s, when the pull was irresistible, this handsome, bright and ambitious lad hopped aboard a molasses boat and traced the Atlantic coast up to the Canada-United States border, to a town he had never heard of, in a corner of some cold and limitless hinterland.

Stepping off that boat changed Sargent's life. It also changed his name. He became "Jiggy the Nigger"—Jiggy to his face.

In St. Stephen, where there were no other black residents at that time, Sargent got a job delivering kerosene on a wagon hitched to a team of horses. House to house he travelled, always grinning and always polite. Everyone knew Jiggy. Why, he was almost like a white person. He even learned to skate—not well, but well enough to play a bit of hockey. Also, on Saturdays and Sundays in his tiny upstairs apartment Sargent hosted the town's most active poker game. From time to time a ballplayer or two dropped in to absorb the ambience of an honest game of chance, or even to sit in for a hand. Sometimes Sargent charged a buck a head; sometimes he would skim the pot. This humble percentage helped supplement the host's weekly stipend, and no one really minded. Besides, there was never a problem at Jiggy's poker games.

Then one year Sargent announced he was going to become a lawyer. People smirked, if they listened at all. But he had had enough of horses and kerosene, and he headed for New England with a few dollars and this incredible notion of attending law school. Somehow he did and, according to the *Saint Croix Courier*, became "a successful practicing attorney around Boston."

One time in the 1930s Sargent returned to St. Stephen for a vacation, going from door to door and from shop to shop "receiving the glad hand everywhere." Even then, few in town knew his real name, but what the hell, Jiggy seemed to have it made.

Several years later a few travellers from St. Stephen pulled into Boston's South Station and noticed a familiar face beneath a red cap, still grinning despite the weight of bags and suitcases.

But this time when Walter Sargent extended his hand, people merely pressed a quarter into his palm and walked away. What became of his promising law career is unclear.

◆   ◆   ◆   ◆

Blacks were a curiosity in St. Stephen, their countenance smiling out from pancake-mix boxes, their wisdom conveyed by men such as heavyweight boxing champion Joe (The Brown Bomber) Louis. The press buttressed this image, perhaps without malice. Still, newspapers oozed racism.

In the *Our Boarding House* cartoon a character named Jason, a slovenly black with voluminous white lips, tells Major Hoople: "Yeowsah, Mistah Majah! Ah cleaned up $147 easy money wif a carnival las' summah—all ah had to do was stick mah haid through a hole in a canvas an' dodge de balls what de customers throwed at me!" These glimpses of the feckless, happy black shaped the perceptions of entire generations of Maritimers.

In areas with a reasonably large black population, interracial ball games dating to the turn of the century spawned teams such as the Halifax Eurekas and the Fredericton Celestials. However, in Maritime communities with few or no blacks, baseball offered inhabitants at least a fleeting opportunity to interact with blacks through the outlandish amalgams of American athletes, entertainers and sluggards known as the barnstorming Negro baseball teams.

From the 1890s until the late 1940s black baseball subsisted across North America on everything from rock-strewn pastures to parks nearly the equal of Yankee Stadium.

The black major leagues, with teams such as the Kansas City Monarchs, the Baltimore Elite Giants and the Birmingham Black Barons, showcased athletes who were denied the full fruits of their magnificent skills. Two of these men, pitcher Satchel Paige and catcher Josh Gibson, were among the best who ever played the sport.

Beneath these elite black teams existed an underclass of clubs comprising players not talented enough, motivated enough or lucky enough to perform with Paige, Gibson and the others. These secondary teams "barnstormed" the continent, bringing a carnival atmosphere to the towns, challenging the local semi-professional and amateur teams, and spicing games with bizarre gimmicks and well-rehearsed routines involving everything from acrobatics to firecrackers.

The Maritimes were fertile ground for American barnstorming teams in the 1930s. There was a decent buck to be had, and conditions afforded a less virulent summer for the black man fleeing the dead-end squalor of the inner city. Some teams booked independently, while others used agents such as the popular Syd Pollack Baseball Agency of North Tarrytown, New York. Each club carried one or two stars whose talents were usually embellished in advance publicity.

Teams beginning the Maritime circuit entered through St. Stephen and played two or three games there before heading off to other baseball centres in New Brunswick, Nova Scotia and Prince Edward Island. Often, they would play another contest or two in St. Stephen on the way home. In total, they would play approximately 30 games in two months. St. Stephen players generally cite regular exposure to these teams as a major source of their own baseball acumen—they termed it "inside baseball"—that helped them win championship after championship. "When you are playing the better teams," reasons St. Stephen outfielder George Purcell, "you are going to play better ball."

And so they landed, saddled with bizarre names and ridiculous costumes, descending upon the rural diamonds as if beamed down from another solar system. Examples are many.

The Zulu Cannibal Giants stripped to the waist, donned wild headdresses and smeared their faces and chests with war paint in the best cinematic interpretation of a cannibal. Approximately 55,000 watched them in a three-game series in Montreal in 1935. The Borneo Zulu Cannibals offered similar fare. The Philadelphia-based Colored Chain Gang performed in convict uniforms and bore monikers such as Speed, Sneak, Stump, Spike, Shine and Yellow Gore. The African Jungle Giants were likely among the seedier operations—if they fulfilled their contract and showed up at all. The

Boston Hoboes, who included white players in the line-up, one year became the Georgia Chain Gang, even though virtually all of the players were from Massachusetts. The Black Shadows warmed up in long, black capes, played in coal-black uniforms and featured Happy Devine, the Clown Prince of Colored Baseball. The Shadows also offered a jitterbug exhibition as standard fare.

Originating in Miami, the Ethiopian Clowns boasted "Chief" Askari, one of the top black pitchers of his day; Spec Bebop, a dwarf; and "King Tut," an adept first baseman. "Tut had a mitt that he could lay eight baseballs in," says Halley Horton, of the Yarmouth Gateways. "Before the game he'd stand there and some guy would deliberately throw the ball low, and Tut would be looking the other way and then he'd stick out his mitt, and the ball would be in it." The team wore full clown attire, including large red wigs and pantaloons, and the Gateways' Lightning Amirault recalls they used to smother ground balls in their suits. As an added attraction, two former Barnum and Bailey circus performers offered brief, stale routines between innings.

The Philadelphia Colored Giants billed themselves as "The World's Colored Champions." They had two major assets: a portable lighting system and Will Jackman. Both cast long shadows.

The portable lighting system allowed St. Stephen to claim to have hosted the first game of night baseball in the Maritimes—on August 29, 1938, against the Colored Giants. (A few other teams also make the same claim, however. But, in any case, St. Stephen won the rain-marred contest 8-4.) A 250-horsepower generator provided the juice for the lighting system. "You could hear the umpires complaining about what a racket the generator was making," says Jim Morell, who pitched the game for St. Stephen. In addition, the Colored Giants brought several poles, each with three or four banks of lights. "The lights were all up on standards, shining down," recalls St. Stephen's, Orville Mitchell. "So you only really hit the top half of the ball. When the ball was coming in on ya, all you could see was a half moon coming in."

Will Jackman was clearly the Giants' star. Tall and relaxed, he was the greatest black pitcher of them all, according to famed black league star Bill Yancey, who played shortstop for eight teams. Jackman was a submarining right-hander from Texas who possessed exquisite control and, in his heyday, great velocity. Newspaper reports claim that in 1927 he won 48 games, lost only four and pitched two no-hitters.

"He could make a ball talk," says St. Stephen's Lefty Brownell. "He had great, big, long fingers and a huge hand. Jackman used to say to me, 'Boy, you sees dem fingas? Dems ma bread and butta an' ain't nobody gonna hurt em.'"

St. Stephen centre fielder Gordon Coffey says that Jackman nattered at every hitter he faced. "You're up there trying to concentrate on the pitch, and he'd be there talking to you all the time. He'd stand there and look at you, and he was about six-foot-four. 'Wha' you gonna do man? I think I know wha' ya gonna try ta do. An' I ain't gonna let ya.' Then he'd call his pitches while they were on the way to home plate. And you'd hear his voice, 'Let it go, let it go. Strike two!'"

From anywhere on the field, Jackman annoyed opponents. He thought it was funny, but some others did not.

"I'm pitching, and Jackman is coaching on third base," recounts St. Stephen pitcher Roy Boles. "And he's hollerin' to the batter, 'Hit un through da box. Hit un through da box.' Then in the eighth inning he came up to bat and I threw one at his head. Just as hard as I could throw it. Down he went on the ground. I didn't hit him, but it was a warning. Then I ran in at him while he was down, and I looked down on him—I could see the whites of his eyes lookin' up at me. I said to him, 'Why don't you hit one through the box?' And he just looked at me. That was the last time he ever hollered at me."

◆　◆　◆　◆

The most respected and important barnstorming team to tour the Maritimes regularly was the Boston Colored Giants. Also known as the Boston Royal Colored Giants or the Boston Royal Giants, the team was owned and managed by catcher Burlin White, a fine athlete and one of the first to use a large catcher's mitt.

White had a privileged upbringing for a black. In his childhood, he had been adopted by a wealthy white family, and he attended college, but it was soon evident that young Burlin's gifts of personality and sagacity made the barnstorming choice a natural one. "He had a smile," black league star Ted Page once said, "that would have made a great public relations man today."

In the Maritimes at least, White *was* a great public relations man.

His garrulousness charmed local newspapermen, who implied fondly that they were his pals. Wrote H. J. Osborne in the *Telegraph-Journal*, "White is one of the most likable team managers that ever piloted an outside team to this city and his coming will be heralded with delight by Saint John fandom."

White's playing career lasted from 1914 to 1942 and included the West Baden Sprudels of Indiana, the Bacharach Giants, the Lincoln Giants, the Philadelphia Royal Stars, the Harrisburg Giants, the Quaker Giants, the Philadelphia Giants and the Cuban Stars. He and Will Jackman were key figures with the Philadelphia Colored Giants, but they split in the early 1930s, White forming his own club.

The Boston Colored Giants were "one of the best uniformed and best equipped teams in the country," proclaimed the *Saint Croix Courier* in 1934. But, in fact, amenities were few. The team's bus served frequently as hotel and restaurant for players and management as they fared to the next town over dusty roads under the stars. Although most Maritime hotels accommodated blacks, granted, begrudgingly in some cases, a shoestring budget made such hospitality moot.

For a few years the Boston Colored Giants featured prime clown Stormy Falk. He was followed by Lefty Southall and then by pitcher Babe Robinson, who had played in Montreal for at least one season. While most of White's players hailed from Boston, one exception was a cocksure lad from Yarmouth, Nova Scotia, named Bucky Berry, who, in a *Courier* snippet entitled "Whitey Imports Darky Hurler," was referred to as "a sturdy boy" and "a Canadian colored chucker."

Despite a regular turnover of players, most thought White omniscient. He was probably in his late 40s or early 50s at mid-decade, and, like most managers in charge of young men travelling from town to town for months at a stretch, White was aware that he was also a surrogate parent. Ballplayers of all races liked to pursue good times on the road, but the mores of the era demanded that blacks both behave well and be seen to be behaving well. White was especially sensitive to this fact, and his scrutiny was unrelenting.

"They weren't drunks or anything. This is a small town, and word would have gotten around pretty quickly," says Doug Horton, of Yarmouth. Adds Lefty Brownell, of St. Stephen, "If one of his players started to slip or get out of line, Burlin White would shoot them right back to Boston and bring another fella right in to take his place."

Of course, complete control was impossible. One day pitcher Babe Robinson, hardly a seafaring sort, decided a boat ride on the St. Croix River was in order. Not far off shore he lost his oars—and his composure—and soon Robinson's screams of distress boomed down the valley. "I don't know how the hell he got out of that one," St. Stephen pitcher Ken Kallenberg says, laughing, "but I know there was quite a stir down there on the river. He didn't know how to row."

The Boston Colored Giants played St. Stephen on a 60-40 basis, with the winner taking the larger percentage of the gate. "One fella told me that the extra 20 percent meant the difference between hot dogs and steak for supper," says Gordon Coffey. The Giants won most of the games but prudently lost just often enough to keep matters interesting and the fans coming out. *Halifax Herald* columnist Alex Nickerson wrote in mid-decade that "it was not necessary that [the Giants] put on the heat from the first pitched ball. They could loaf along, confident of their ability to push across enough runs in the last two innings to win handily."

Whatever their concerns about the score, the Giants' stock in trade remained entertainment, and one of their primary vehicles was a pantomime known as shadow baseball. "It looked so real," remembers Lloyd Young, of the Liverpool Larrupers, "you'd swear they were throwing something between them, it was that good. They'd play their positions, and the guy on second base would throw down to third, and that guy would slap his mitt as if the ball was goin' in it. They had it down to perfection."

Clowning was not always appreciated, however.

"When I played ball, I played to win," says Laurie Thorborne, a Larrupers pitcher. "Comedy would offset my pitching. They'd hold the bat, and instead of tryin' to hit with it, the batter would just point it towards the ball. It looked like he was tryin' to show me up. Once, I threw a close ball to him to see what he was doin', and I split his finger right in two."

Yarmouth's Halley Horton remembers one time when Nate Bain was on second base and was attempting to advance on a deep fly ball when the Giants' second baseman jokingly clutched Bain's ankle.

"Nate squared off and hit him so quick you wouldn't believe it. And his fella, realizin' that Nate wasn't foolin' around, backed right off. Burlin White walked out and balled the fellow out. 'What are you doin' out here? You know better than that!' He didn't say a word to Nate. But that's the way Burlin controlled his team."

Good-natured banter was part of their playing persona as well. Says Al Young, of the Larrupers, "They talked from the time they got on the field until they left."

Often this talk was instructional, and Lloyd Young of Liverpool says White gave it freely, relishing his role as travelling tutor to the amateurs. Young was shown how to position his foot properly on the bag, while teammate Garneau Seaman says White taught him how to kick the ball out of an opponent's glove when sliding into a base. "Once, he lost a game by me kicking the ball out of his hands in the late innings. 'White boy,' he said, 'I taught you how to kick the ball, but I didn't mean against me!'"

White was close to the Seaman family of Liverpool, a unit that included four brothers and their father, Papa John Seaman. After games in Liverpool, White would visit with the elder Seaman in a back room of the family's clothing store. Players sat hushed as the affable White held the small assembly spellbound—recounting his experiences and impressions and dispensing tips until two or three o'clock in the morning. No charge.

◆　◆　◆　◆

Even amid such curious brethren, the House of David was peculiar. Easily the best of the white barnstorming teams, the House of David was an enduring enigma because of a whispered religious connection fostered by the players' long hair, ragged beards and seemingly divine baseball skills.

The team was based in an 800-acre religious colony in Benton Harbor, Michigan, which was located on the shores of Lake Michigan about 100 miles from Chicago. The colony had been founded in 1903 by 42-year-old Benjamin Purnell, a former devotee of a zealot named Michael Keyfor Mills, who proclaimed that, just as Eve had seduced Adam into sin, he would seduce women into virtue. Purnell professed to be the younger brother of Jesus Christ, and his followers claimed a bloodline to the lost tribes of Israel. Purnell promised immortality in an earthly paradise to celibate vegetarian non-smokers who did not drink, shave or cut their hair. Naturally, all of their worldly goods went to the colony.

The success of fruit-growing and canning operations on the colony spawned offshoots such as a travelling band, a baseball team and, finally, a theme park. By the 1920s the sect had 900 members, and a House of David was established in Australia.

However, one of the great scandals of the decade, however, would eat away at membership. Indicted for rape in 1922, Purnell disappeared for four years. When he finally turned up for his trial in 1926, the court found that he had used the House of David for personal gain and to cover acts such as debauching several young girls. Purnell died of tuberculosis shortly afterwards, and the colony continued, though damaged in spirit and supply.

By 1936, as the House of David ball team traversed the Maritimes, the colony had dwindled to 167 members. It was an inordinately small pool from which to draw such a proficient baseball team—a point newspapers across the region overlooked willingly. In truth, not all of the players were from the colony, and indeed, at one point all but two of the players were outsiders.

The team travelled with a 25,000-candlepower lighting system, worth in 1930s dollars more than $30,000. Five trucks transported the lighting system and an entourage of approximately 30 men. The team also employed comedians, chief among them Beardless Hammon and Keats Marzulli—the latter did impersonations of the umpire and of home-town players. Another feature had House of David players standing shoulder-to-shoulder, the first man dropping a coin, kicking it, catching it, dropping it again, then kicking it to the next fellow, and so on. The routine went faster and faster and mesmerized local ballplayers as much as it did spectators.

The House of David was a partner in one of the most improbable unions in the history of sport, when the legendary Grover Cleveland Alexander was appointed manager. Affectionately called Ol' Pete, Alexander had been one of the greatest pitchers ever. He was also a war-traumatized epileptic whose alcoholism hastened his release from at least two major league teams that feared his undesirable ways would corrupt younger players. In his latter years, Alexander's progressed to the point where his wife was forced to hide her perfume so he would not drink it. He ended up working for a flea circus and died alone in 1950 in a boarding house.

But before his sad ending, Alexander turned up with the House of David one day in 1931, yakking with reporters who nodded gratefully at even his most insipid statements.

"I made it a point to insist that I would not have to grow a beard when I took over the management of this team," he told one American newspaperman. "First of all, I wasn't sure if I could grow a beard. Never having grown one before I would have felt mighty ashamed had I been contracted to sprout whiskers and then been forced to glue some to my face. Then there was the possibility that if I succeeded in growing said beard, my friends would be unable to recognize me. Or that I would not recognize myself for that matter. So I decided against it. Sure I had a battle with the elders of Benton Harbor to see things my way. Evidently though they caved in and now 25 cents extra per day is deducted from the gate receipts so that I may have my morning shave. Great, what?"

Later, the team's rules concerning facial hair were relaxed slightly, remembers Gordon Coffey, of the St. Croixs. "They had this young fellow without a beard, and the crowd was yellin' at him until he finally stood up and took off his cap, and down fell his long, braided hair right down to his shoulders."

Appearances aside, several House of David players were near major league calibre. A 26-year-old pitcher from South Dakota, Allen Wilbert (Bullet Ben) Benson pitched 10 disappointing innings in 1934 for the Washington Senators, of the American League. "It is said," reported the *Halifax Chronicle*, "that on ladies day Allen spends many minutes brushing and combing his luxuriant whiskers." The Brooklyn Dodgers owned the rights to centre fielder George Klaus, and Shoeless Joe Jackson, a key figure in the infamous Black Sox Scandal of 1919, was rumored to have played third base briefly for the House of David. Among the most esteemed to wear their colors was the greatest woman athlete of her era, Babe Didrikson, who could reportedly throw a baseball more than 300 feet.

"One time, they brought their whole infield in," recalls Doug Horton, of the Yarmouth Gateways, "and we didn't even get a ball out there. We knew when they played a game they could practically name the score.... They were that good."

◆　◆　◆　◆

Business ethics and bizarre appearances aside, most of the barnstorming teams were more successful and lasted much longer in the 1930s than did Saint John's forays into semi-professional baseball. And in 1937, the city was at it again. The first attempt had vaporized like a morning fog when the club, called the Saint Johns, withdrew in 1931 after their second season in the Boston Twilight League. Now, in 1937, greying local heroes were summoned and novices were recruited from as far away as Boston. Although hardly a fraternity of the famous, they at least hinted at respectability.

The player atop the wish list of Saint John manager Ray Hansen was St. Stephen's Cecil (Lefty) Brownell. Whispering sweet nothings into Brownell's ego and promising fresh green in his palm, Hansen persuaded the southpaw to attend what was known euphemistically as training camp, and in mid-June scheduled him to pitch an exhibition game against the St. Croixs.

Alas, the game never happened because the team never happened.

After much press ballyhoo and before a roster had been finalized, the team folded after two weeks. Promoters had decided that "the undertaking was too great an expense and gamble," the *Telegraph-Journal* explained tersely.

For Brownell, it was a close call. He had been within two days of signing with the semi-pro team, a move which, according to the pitcher, would have "buggered my amateur." Brownell, still pure, soon returned to the St. Croixs.

The St. Stephen St. Croixs were gentries of Maritime amateur baseball in 1937. Ken Kallenberg was overpowering opposition, striking out 15 in one game, hitting at will and now reaching his prime. Centre fielder Gordon Coffey was developing into a team leader with a glowing Maritime reputation. Meanwhile, catcher Muddy McLain was still depleting the first-aid kit regularly.

"When McLain was hit by a pitch in the sixth it was feared for a minute that the injury would be serious," reported the *Courier.* "The sphere caught him on the skull with a resounding crack as he was ducking away from an inside ball. But while spectators gasped in amazement he took a turn or two around the plate and a healthy swig and continued in the game with no apparent injury."

In the first game of the 1937 New Brunswick finals, St. Stephen beat the Saint John Pontiacs 4-1 behind Brownell's five-hitter. The offensive epicentre, though, lay in the bat of second baseman Sweet Pea McCarroll, who had four hits and drove in all of St. Stephen's runs. "St. Stephen's little package of dynamite," said the *Telegraph-Journal.*

More than any other amateur ballplayer—except, perhaps, Yarmouth's Halley Horton—the press embraced tiny, fiery-eyed Phil McCarroll. They dubbed him "Sweet Pea" after the Popeye comic-strip character, marvelled at his quickness and savoured his enthusiasm.

Well into his 20s, McCarroll remained the Rockwellian youngster with a bat and a glove in a cow pasture, learning to catch and throw and realizing that, with *his* size, intelligence must be his closest athletic ally. As a mite, he had fought until dark for fly balls with a dozen other extended mitts, sliding and running and sharing in the unbridled delight that comes from cavorting in a cow pasture with a bat and a glove.

An excellent student who was seemingly destined for community leadership, McCarroll was also the unanimous choice for the Reverend J. W. Holland prize—$10—for athletic excellence at St. Joseph's College in Moncton, New Brunswick. He graduated from St. Joseph's with a bachelor of arts degree with honors, and he was class president.

In 1930 his father bought a restaurant in St. Stephen that included four tables, four sets of chairs, a lunch counter, a glass showcase and a glass pie case. Whatever its material shortcomings, it was a comfortable enclave. A coal stove warmed the main dining area, and each morning a new fire crackled. The cook stayed for 30 years, asking only for Tuesday afternoons off to shop in Calais and get her hair done. It came to be called Phil's Cafe, a town shrine for good talk and good food. The doors opened at 7 a.m. sharp, and by 7:30 the regulars were in their usual places.

"We did a helluva good business," says McCarroll. "We got all the farmers. We sold meals for 40 cents, and a piece of pie for 10 cents. We served mostly fried food, hamburgers cooked on a gas stove, and oyster stew. Dr. Brownrigg would be the first man in in the morning. He didn't say a thing, and the cook fed him. She'd have strawberries and cream for him, and maybe give him a fried egg. He paid us, but he never charged her a bill when she went to see him."

Outsiders were also welcome at Phil's Cafe. Gordie Drillon, Toronto Maple Leaf star and NHL scoring champion, dropped in every now and then to see his friend Phil.

In baseball, McCarroll was groomed by the St. Stephen Blue Caps, a short-lived intermediate team. It was a valuable training ground, and it taught the value of patience.

"You couldn't break into the St. Croixs," says McCarroll. "They had their nine men—bing, bing, bing—and those were their nine men. They wouldn't take you if you were just as good. You had to be better, and it was hard to be better than those fellas."

At second base, McCarroll studied hitters, moved with every pitch and positioned himself astutely—often so deeply that an opponent once barked, "I wish the Christ you'd play the infield instead of the outfield." He and the St. Croixs' volatile shortstop, Rainnie Moffatt, were a wondrous duo, as compatible on the diamond as they were dissimilar off.

Genteel and religious—other players tempered their language around him—McCarroll was a natural counterpoint to the team's constant cut-up, Squirrelly Ross.

Still, even McCarroll capitulated occasionally to temptation, once trying a plug of chewing tobacco. A few seconds and a few chomps later, however, he spat out the whole foul mass. Deviance had a terrible taste for Sweet Pea.

"He was the most even-tempered person on the ball field," says teammate Jim Morell. "He was always encouraging people. If he thought a fella was getting down, he [would] come over and pat them on the back and say somethin' foolish. He was good that way."

At five-foot-five and 120 pounds, McCarroll revered competition and loved to win.

One time, while returning from an exhibition game in Bar Harbor, Maine, he and Kallenberg jibed one another for miles about who was the better athlete. The discussion intensified until, in the middle of nowhere, McCarroll cried out suddenly, "Stop the car!" The pair leapt out to settle the issue—with a foot race.

"It was about seven or eight o'clock at night, gettin' dark," says McCarroll. "We got right out on the road and measured off 30 or 40 yards. I was supposed to be pretty fast, but I was just startin' when he was finishin'. We got back in the car and went a little farther and we came to a lake in the Cherryfield Woods. I said, 'You can run fast, but by God, Kallenberg, I can swim fast.'"

Kallenberg smiled. "Stop the car!" he said.

Again the players alighted and, on the side of the road, stripped to the buff, all in the name of athletic rank.

"I thought I could swim because once I won a contest in Ottawa. So we swam maybe 30 yards," says McCarroll.

"He was just startin' when I hit the other shore," recalls Kallenberg.

It was the last time Sweet Pea McCarroll ever challenged Ken Kallenberg.

◆　◆　◆　◆

Without catcher Muddy McLain, who had a split right thumb, and centre fielder Gordon Coffey, who was suffering with a charley horse, St. Stephen still beat the Saint John Pontiacs 7-1 in the second game of the New Brunswick final to take a 2-0 lead in the series. The decisive blow was Phil McCarroll's third-inning, two-run homer. "It went out through shortstop and it just rolled and rolled and rolled," he recalls. It was the only home run of the New Brunswick playoffs that year, and it earned McCarroll a wool sweater, compliments of a St. Stephen clothing dealer. The St. Croixs finished off the Pontiacs the following day and earned their seventh consecutive provincial championship.

The title was by now a late-summer rite.

The victory set up another meeting with the Yarmouth Gateways, who had beaten St. Stephen in 1935 and briefly taken the Maritime title away from them. "This year it will be a different team that faces Yarmouth," wrote H. J. Osborne in the *Telegraph-Journal*. "According to all reports there will be no night life. Everybody will be in bed and ready for the morrow...."

Around Yarmouth, the '37 Gateways were christened "The Miracle Team." Coach Ernie Grimshaw had nurtured younger players and galvanized veterans. In the latter category were 40-year-old outfielder Murray (Papa) Veno, who hit .346, and pitcher Copie LeBlanc, who led the team at .457. "From the manager on down the boys are one happy family," reported the *Halifax Herald*.

In St. Stephen for game one, more than 2,000 fans spilled over the grandstands and down the foul lines to watch the St. Croixs win 4-3. Third baseman Nate Bain's throwing error in the first inning was the contest's key play, igniting an early St. Croix rally. Typical of Yarmouth-St. Stephen finals, the game hissed and rumbled with a malevolent undercurrent that surfaced when a LeBlanc curve ball nailed centre fielder Coffey on the back of the head, flattening and dazing the St. Stephen star. Coffey eventually arose unhurt.

The loss in game one enraged the tenacious Grimshaw, who warned his players, "I want tomorrow's game at any cost."

Nevertheless, the next day Gordon Coffey's single, double and triple helped crush the Gateways, 12-5. Down in the series two games to one, the Miracle Team now had to match its name. *Halifax Chronicle* columnist Ace Foley suggested that the Gateways might start ace LeBlanc in three straight games, reasoning, "Copie is the only pitcher in the Maritimes today likely to succeed in such an improbable feat."

In game three, LeBlanc and Ken Kallenberg duelled in the sun, hitless until the third and scoreless until the seventh, when LeBlanc scored on Doug Horton's triple. With a 1-0 Yarmouth lead, with just two innings remaining, with LeBlanc pitching magnificently, and with the screams and the hopes of the home crowd eddying up to the heavens, it appeared that the Gateways would at least prolong the series.

Then, in the eighth inning, St. Stephen threatened. With Art Lowe on third, Grimshaw intentionally walked St. Croixs' outfielder Dana Miles—a late-session addition from Calais—putting runners on first and third and bringing to the fore Sweet Pea McCarroll.

It was reasonable strategy, not only because the move set up a force out at second base, but because it summoned to the plate the diminutive second baseman who was enduring the worst game of a personally disappointing series. McCarroll had struck out on three pitches in the first inning, had feebly grounded out to third in the third inning and had tapped back to the pitcher in the sixth. Zero for three.

Knowing that he was vastly overmatched against the mighty Acadian southpaw, McCarroll—with two on and two out in the eighth inning of a Maritime final game, before thousands of eyes and a score of newspapermen—froze.

Persuading his feet to take him towards home plate, he abruptly circled back and ran to Baldy Moffatt. The coach lowered his head and listened.

"Look, Baldy," McCarroll pleaded, "put somebody else up in my place. You know I haven't been hittin'."

Moffatt stepped in closer to his player. "Just put your bat on the ball, that's all you have to do. Just put your bat on the ball."

Moffatt turned away, and McCarroll winced and headed for the plate.

Sweet Pea watched the first pitch go by, and the bat did not leave his shoulder. Strike one.

The next pitch was a low, wide curve that McCarroll missed by a foot, accenting the futile lunge by tipping forward onto the balls of his feet. Strike two.

Then came the third pitch.

"It was just one of those things that you dream about," McCarroll says. "He pitched, and it was a third strike, so I swung and it went out over the third baseman's head. I don't know how I did it."

McCarroll slid into second, as Lowe and Miles dashed home. St. Stephen led, and eventually won, 2-1.

The victory that gave St. Stephen its sixth Maritime championship in seven years ended more than just a baseball series: it humbled Copie LeBlanc.

In the bottom of the ninth with one out, LeBlanc had walked, then moved to second on a hit batter. With the Yarmouth crowd awakening the heavens, LeBlanc, the tying run, moved off the base as Kallenberg delivered. Whack! The ball shot back at the pitcher, who stuck out his glove for the second out, then spun alertly and threw to second, catching LeBlanc off the base for the third out. Double play. Game over.

It was an ignominious ending for the great LeBlanc, who had pitched a two-hitter and scored his team's only run that day. None of that mattered, however, as he arose slowly from the infield dust and watched the stands empty quietly. If redemption was necessary, he would never get the chance. This was the last Yarmouth-St. Stephen final.

Nor would there be any requite for LeBlanc the citizen, the arrogant outsider. Two years later, he would slip out of Yarmouth under a cloud, his reputation ruined because funds from a local ice cream company for which he worked as an accountant were inexplicably missing.

No charges were laid.

LEFTY LEVELS LIVERPOOL

"If they send in Specs Brownell, he'll get pasted."
—Ace Foley—

A S THE WORLD acquainted itself in 1938 with civilian gas masks and other accoutrements of war, the St. Croix Valley quietly watched folks go by. Hordes crossed the Ferry Point Bridge connecting contented and sociable St. Stephen with Calais. The *Saint Croix Courier* would report the total number of crossings in a year to be six million—this total including the locals who crossed the bridge several times daily. Of course, some of those crossings were more adventurous than others.

"[A] French-Canadian resident of Moncton who came through last week from the United States [was] passed by the officers on duty during the night shift," said the *Courier*. "Some time afterward in the wee small hours of the morning when there was little or no traffic, the men heard a scratching noise at the door ... and on investigation found the Moncton man attempting to make an entrance. When he first saw the officer his first reaction was, 'Where am I, Moncton?' Then recognizing the same men who had examined his car a few hours before he bellowed, 'What, you here too?' It was some time before the officers could convince him that he was back in St. Stephen. It seems that after leaving the bridge here he turned the wheel over to his daughter and as he was snatching a little sleep she drove into St. Andrews and back again to the bridge. When he finally realized that he had lost 40 miles or more his anger, to put it mildly, knew no bounds."

Other visitors attracted attention without saying a word.

"Port officials and bystanders at the International Bridge were treated to an unusual sight Monday night when the Godino Siamese twins passed on their way to Sydney, N.S.," the *Courier* reported. "The twins are male and from casual observation somewhere in their 20s. They are joined at the hip. Both are married and had their wives with them. Amazingly active and apparently but little inconvenienced by what most people would term an affliction but what may be a source of considerable income to them, they attracted a big crowd, most of which, like the writer, was viewing the phenomenon for the first time."

Pitcher Ken Kallenberg, too, was on the move. The right-handed pitcher was spotted by the Boston Red Sox organization and by April was on his way to a tryout camp in Little Rock, Arkansas.

His departure left the St. Croixs with a large void, so the baseball committee reached out once more, this time to Jim Morell, a lanky six-foot-three, tautly muscled veteran from the Miramichi region of New Brunswick.

Jim Morell was outgoing, always fit, and, wrote the *Courier*, he had a character "above reproach." It was this last quality that the St. Croixs and, indeed, the town portrayed as a major prerequisite.

Soon after joining the team in 1938, he was one of the most popular players, teaching Sunday school and dating Vera Webber, a bright and attractive daughter of team manager, Len Webber. The two would eventually marry.

More to the point, however, this man of high moral fibre was also the decade's pre-eminent Maritime mound mercenary—an arm hired out by Newcastle, Grand Falls, Newcastle again, Saint John, Westville, Minto and St. Stephen.

His road to the border town had been circuitous and fraught with apprenticeships that had tested his love for the sport and his patience with himself.

"Baseball was something I had to sneak away to do," he says of the early days. "On a nice day, if we were hayin', I'd figure all day how I'd get to that game tonight, because I had to pitch at seven o'clock. And there was no just goin' up sayin' that I had to play ball that night. There was hay to get in. Jeepers! You just didn't do it. Anyway, people sort of took a dim view of people who were in sports. In my day, it seemed that hockey players and baseball players were people who had nothin' to do."

Morell started his senior career in 1926 with Newcastle. There, he carried railway ties all day, rushed home after work to gulp down a glass of milk, walked a couple of miles to the ball park, pitched, then walked home. Seldom was there cash or coaching.

"The fans used to say, 'Only girls throw underhand.' I thought they were makin' fun of me. The manager? He'd come up to ya and ask, 'How ya doing?' and he'd be shakin' all over himself. No one ever came to me and said, for example, that I was going to pitch in Springhill tomorrow and that I was not going to have a friend in the stands. That they were going to be hollering dirty, rotten things at me, and for it not to let it get me down."

Often he pitched back-to-back games. In Grand Falls, where he was paid $21 a week to pitch, he once threw seven games in nine days. He endured a similar string in Westville. "I guess they figured that I was being paid, and if they said that you were going to pitch, well, you were going to pitch."

Yet Morell never protested. He didn't know why he should. He was playing ball, wasn't he?

He had labored entire winters and had earned less than $21 for the lot. "I would work all winter, and I wouldn't make $21 the whole winter. I worked for 50 cents a day. Then, for somebody to come along and offer to pay me to play ball.... They were always after pitchers, and pitchers could ask for a few bucks. If somebody offered you more money to play for their team and you figured they had a better team and a better chance to win, you moved to that team," Morell explains.

His best pitch was the submarine, a baffling, whipping delivery that sent the ball on labyrinthine inclines to home plate. "I threw it underhand and scraped my knuckles on the ground doing it," Morell once told a reporter about the pitch he had learned from a book. "The way it rose made it hard for the hitters."

The passing years, however, had improved the hitters' chances considerably. By the time he played his first game in a St. Stephen uniform, his fastball had slowed and his curve had straightened. Morell was 31.

Pitching was interspersed with jobs such as the one he was given wheeling cement after joining the Saint John Trumps. "I upset two or three wheelbarrows, and everybody would hoot and holler and laugh. Then I'd get mad. I just couldn't do it." So they gave him a pick and shovel.

Given that sort of existence, meals were titanic events in Morell's life. The player whom fans had once dubbed "Old Shad Bones," because he could afford to eat little more than shad and bony gaspereau, looked forward to free meals on the road.

"With St. Stephen, there'd be 16 on the trip ... and they would never figure on why there'd be 19 meals charged up. Well, Ken Kallenberg and I were always starving. We'd get the girl to bring us two roast chickens, three glasses of milk. If we could get away with it, we'd do it. In those days I was supposed to be able to eat more than three or four of them on the ball team. I was *always* hungry. Then, we had to go out later and get a lunch." Morell's appetite was a matter of public record. Once, when he returned to Newcastle for a few days to help at his parents' home, the *Courier* scoffed, "Those who have seen him eat will question whether that is a help or a hindrance."

The St. Croixs paid Morell approximately $25 a week to tend the ball diamond—a lark compared with his former tasks. Although he claimed at the time that whitewashing the flag pole in centre field was the hardest work he had ever done, few sympathized. Team management called him the chief carpenter, and he tapped away at the bleachers and combed the grounds, sometimes aided by other ballplayers, often alone.

But Jim Morell never protested.

◆ ◆ ◆ ◆

The team underwent several other roster changes in 1938, also adding pitchers Grant Allen and Donald Norton—a teenage whippet from Milltown, New Brunswick. At mid-season, Ken Kallenberg returned from the Red Sox affiliate in Arkansas for what would be his final season with the St. Croixs. Dana Miles, a superb outfielder from Calais; Cliff Middlemiss, a utility player; and Charlie Weatherby, a big first baseman, all made the team, while outfielder Squirrelly Ross packed it in after five seasons.

A shuffle also took place at catcher: Theo (Muddy) McLain retired and Charlie Godfrey became the team's starter. Godfrey's understudy for the remainder of the decade would be the green but talented Lloyd Kelly. The youngster—who had followed the ball team since his mid-teens, hanging around after games looking for discarded balls and broken bats—found that being a member of the unit required more than baseball skills. "They were a little clannish by this time because they had been together so long," says Kelly. "I was just a kid, and it was hard to break into that gang, into that crowd."

For the departing McLain, one of the original Mohawks, retirement ended a storied succession of lacerations, lesions, cuts, gashes, stitches, concussions, bumps, swellings, fractures, stubbed toes, nicks, twists and shiners. His had been seven sore summers.

In 1932, he chased a foul ball square into third baseman Harry Boles, the latter dropping the ball while the former lay for several minutes on the field. A doctor soon ordered McLain to the bench, stitched up a gash over his right eyelid, then sent him back into the field. In 1933, he twisted his ankle twice during practice. In 1934, while running into the wire in front of the grandstand after a foul fly, he stepped into a hole and again wrenched his left ankle. In 1935, he again crashed into some wire and ended his season. In early 1938, McLain was blinded by the sun and missed a pop-up, the ball's landing opening a large gash over his left eye. Blood gushed from the cut. And so on.

His burly frame belied a quiet, sensitive man with a college education and an enduring shyness—a manifestation of his life-long stutter. "He'd be telling you this story," says Gordon Coffey, "and he'd get right down to the punchline and you didn't want to laugh before he gave you the punchline, but...."

"It was funny that he stuttered when he talked about certain things," recalls Ken Kallenberg. "Other things, he'd come right out with it."

The topic of women regularly brought his impediment to the surface. "Of course, Theo never really had a girl at all," says Orville Mitchell. "There was this married woman who used to go to all the games, and she was pretty friendly with Theo, but that might not have been much. He finally married a girl [in 1939] that was 10 to 12 years younger. But, as far as I know, he never went with anybody. And that was because of his stuttering. It was embarrassing for him. All he did was play baseball. Never bowled, never played pool. And he sang."

McLain was part of a team quartet that featured several players through the years including Orville Mitchell, Ike Vanstone, Charlie Godfrey and George Lee. "We had quite a following throughout the Maritimes," says Mitchell. During playoffs the quartet, which never had an official name, sang for radio audiences in Saint John and Yarmouth. When McLain sang, his stutter disappeared.

Not surprisingly, he was a reliable, even-tempered catcher with a good throwing arm and superb judgment. The press called him "a field general." McLain appreciated the label.

◆ ◆ ◆ ◆

In the 1938 provincial semi-finals, Lefty Brownell was the winning pitcher in all three games as St. Stephen swept past Fredericton-Devon, champions of the York-Sunbury League. The provincial finals were a sterner test. The St. Croixs lost game one 1-0 to the Saint Johns and to 17-year-old "Wonder Boy" Johnny Harvey, who yielded just four hits. Brownell yielded just three hits. St. Stephen won games two and three behind Morell and Kallenberg respectively, Gordon Coffey homering in game three.

In game four, more than 2,000 Saint Johners watched starters Bill Damery and Brownell go head to head in the year's most anticipated match-up. After four tight innings the St. Croixs led just 2-1.

Then Gordon Coffey reached for a bat.

Gifted and graceful, educated and eloquent, poised and patrician of bearing, Coffey was an exemplary man of the 1930s. He seemed to possess life's golden touch.

Of average height, slim build and delicately featured face, Coffey was a versatile sportsman. He tended goal for the Mount Allison University hockey team, played football and rugby, and coached the St. Stephen High School girls' basketball team to the Maritime championship in 1938.

He was the youngest of five sons of a St. Stephen farmer. His mother pined for at least one son to become a minister, but none did. The most pressure was exerted on young Gordon, who, in the end, chose teaching for his life's work.

Coffey had a personality characterized by caution. Some team-mates called him aloof. Whereas they would cuss and shout, Coffey's emotions seemed forever in check, making him difficult to read. Still, he was the epitome of sportsmanship and one of the few players compatible with the bellicose coach, Baldy Moffatt. "(Gordon) didn't play around," says Sweet Pea McCarroll. "Didn't do much drinkin' or anything like that. He wasn't rowdy. He was conservative, and he would speak his mind."

Coffey joined the St. Stephen senior baseball team—then called the Mohawks—in 1931. He was 20 years old and was the team's weakest hitter, admittedly "hanging on to the coat-tails of the older fellas." He was always among the swiftest, though, and his glowing fielding skills seemed innate. Wrote the *Courier* early in the decade: "If the ball is hit anywhere in the centre garden ... chances are a hundred to one that the flying feet of Gordon Coffey will carry this speedy youngster to a spot immediately under it in about the same time that the Midnight Express could cover the same distance on a cylinder track."

He says the existence of a semi-pro league in the area guided him into the outfield when he was still in junior high school. "Those fellas used to go out to the ball field and have batting practice in the morning," Coffey recalls. "I thought I was having great fun chasing those fly balls for the big ballplayers, and they were tickled to death to have some kid out there to chase the balls. I learned a lot by chasing fly balls that way."

His pre-eminent defensive skill was throwing—accurate, consistent rockets. "Gordon Coffey had the best arm of anybody I've ever seen," says outfielder Squirrelly Ross. "He could be out there in the outfield, and that ball wouldn't be six feet high when it left him and it went clean into the plate."

"Nobody liked to stand out on the mound and throw batting practice," says Coffey, "but I liked to stand out there. It would strengthen the arm. I didn't have size or the strength of the bigger players, but there was a knack. If people [were] on base, I never stood under a fly ball and waited for it to come down. I was a step or two back, and at the last moment, I would step into the ball. And I was all ready to throw when it hit my glove. And that saved a couple of steps on the base runner."

Reputation made a great arm even greater. "When I was in college I hurt my shoulder playing football. And every once in a while, when I was sliding into a base, I'd put my hand down and I'd injure the shoulder again. It would be days before I could put that arm back to where I could throw. I never told anybody that, and nobody ever caught me flat-footed. But there were days when we were playing when I threw the ball back into the infield underhanded. No one ever caught on."

The skinny youth who began the decade at the bottom of the batting order was, by decade's end, hitting clean-up and leading his team in average. It was no accident. On summer days while teammates worked, the schoolteacher prevailed upon students to pitch batting practice to him. He hit right, swung a 36-inch bat—longer than that of most major leaguers—and feasted off left-handers who dared curve him outside. With the long bat and the outside pitch, most of Coffey's hits fell to earth in right field.

By 1938 Gordon Coffey was unquestionably without peer on the St. Croixs. "Coffey was the star," says Kallenberg. "It didn't make any difference if he was out there playing on the field, or out on the street."

◆ ◆ ◆ ◆

As Saint John's Bill Damery threw his final warm-up pitches to start the sixth inning of game four, Coffey, his team up 2-1, stood on deck taking a few practice swings and struggling to focus on baseball. Like most unmarried men of the era, he could not help thinking about a possible world war.

"I was in the militia at the time and I was getting kind of anxious about things," Coffey recalls. "The prime minister of Great Britain had just been over talking with Hitler and had come back and said peace in our time. I was standing [on deck] there, and a kid came by selling newspapers. He had a bag full. I remember saying to him, 'Johnny, what does it say?' And he held up the paper, and there it was in big letters, four inches high: PEACE. This was a mental relief all of a sudden, like a shot of cocaine or something, I suppose."

Moments later a relieved Coffey knocked Damery's second pitch, a chest-high curve, over the left-field fence for a home run.

St. Stephen won 3-2 and captured an incredible eighth straight provincial title.

As the St. Croixs were accomplishing that, the Liverpool Larrupers were claiming their first Nova Scotia title. Perennial whipping boys to the Yarmouth Gateways and the Springhill Fence Busters, the Larrupers of 1938 were doormats no longer.

A passionate town on the ocean's edge, Liverpool, Nova Scotia, thrived at the mouth of the Mersey River, 70 miles southwest of Halifax. Since its founding in the mid-1700s, the town had cultivated a kingly reputation for building, repairing and worshipping seafaring objects. In the 1930s, the town had 2,700 inhabitants, mostly of English extraction but with pockets of Scottish, Dutch and German descendants—a volatile mix contained by a one-man police force on a bicycle.

Townsfolk had money then, illegal money from rumrunning and legitimate money from the Mersey Paper Company, the town's largest employer. A woodcutter, for example, could earn $80 a month, plus board. It was an excellent income for the time.

Perhaps the most piteous thing about Liverpool was its baseball team. Forget that "larruper" meant fighter. Luckless and leaderless, the early 1930s were forbidding times for the baseball club. The players chalked up more errors than hits, and a win a month was a goal not always realized. As the decade matured, however, so did the Larrupers, and the town that had supported losers positively swooned for its winners.

"Every time we played ball, they'd close the stores," says pitcher Laurie Thorborne. "Everybody would be goin' over to the ball park. There'd be hundreds and hundreds and hundreds, and they came from all over—Lunenburg, Bridgewater, Shelburne, all over. They'd fill the park right up.... And you'd come back after a ball game out of town and you'd get in at 12 midnight, and the town would be filled, waitin'. We had a lovely ball town."

Coached by R. H. (Raw) Murray, a stern schoolteacher of comparatively limited baseball grasp, the team was anchored by two sets of brothers, the Youngs and the Seamans. The Youngs included first baseman Lloyd, outfielder Al and third baseman Bert.

The four Seaman boys, of Arabian descent, were perhaps the best-known sporting family in the Maritimes. The oldest was pitcher Ike, called the Iron Man because of his stellar effort in a 14-inning contest in Yarmouth earlier in the decade. "Ike was a nervous player," says teammate Thorborne. "I seen him up in Yarmouth one day, he was supposed to pitch, and we had to take him back to the hotel four times because he had diarrhea or somethin'." Ike studied players carefully, always looking for an edge. He once wrote a letter to Joe Cronin, manager of the Boston Red Sox and later president of the American League, describing two players in detail and asking which would be the most dangerous batter. Cronin replied, "If a man steps to the plate dressed in a baseball uniform with a bat in his hand, that's the most dangerous batter."

Shortstop Killem, the youngest Seaman brother, was talented and studious. The latter quality would enable "Kal" to become head of orthopedic surgery at Saint John Regional Hospital, and a member of the legislature in the Liberal government of New Brunswick premier Frank McKenna.

The middle brothers, outfielders Danny and Garneau, were also accomplished. After his playing days Danny was a highly successful provincial coach, and recently Liverpool honored his life's work by naming its new baseball facility Danny Seaman Park. Garneau managed Canadian light-heavyweight and heavyweight champion Terrance (Tiger) Warrington. Garneau says people were skeptical when he signed Warrington, who was black, but Garneau ignored the doubters and oversaw the boxer's training regime, which included workouts in an old barn and daily runs along nearby Summerville Beach.

A fifth brother, Fosh, played briefly. The patriarch was John Seaman, a gregarious merchant known for lavishing Lebanese feasts on visiting ballplayers and journalists.

Apart from Ike Seaman, other Larruper pitchers included right-hander Thorborne, the intense ace, and Fred Kenney, a mercurial left-hander whose "dipsy-doo" pitch—a quasi-knuckleball—caused batters as much anxiety as his drinking caused his teammates. Liverpool journalist Armond Wigglesworth says that Kenney had two pitches, the dipsy-doo and a slider. "When he was able to work his dipsy-doo ball, they'd swing over their heads after it. But it was not a pitch to build a career on." Pitcher Jim Mont, who joined Liverpool in 1939, remembers Kenney as being quite a drinker. "In St. Stephen we were rained out for a few days, and every day we went across the bridge to Calais. We'd be walking by a tavern, and there'd be this tap on the window, and there'd be Freddie, sittin' all by himself with all these bottles of beer around him."

Liverpool became the Nova Scotia champions following a bitter, six-game final with the Halifax Capitals, truculent veterans coached by former International Leaguer, Steamer Lucas. The clinching game was a one-hit 12-2 masterpiece by Thorborne, who faced just 29 batters. Ironically, post-game celebrations were marred by the player largely responsible for the rejoicing, catcher Nelson Deveau.

Nelson (Zoomie) Deveau was 27 years old in 1938, and his thick, six-foot-one, 170-pound physique was at its peak. A hopeless third baseman, he caught his first game for the Yarmouth Gateways when catcher Pete White showed up drunk. By the time White sobered up, he had lost his position. A few years later, Liverpool lured Deveau from Yarmouth with a job in the Mersey paper mill. It seems that the mill superintendent was a ball fan.

Although welcomed gleefully by his new Liverpool teammates, Deveau's arrival was perilous for Larruper pitchers unaccustomed to his rocket throws to second base. Previously, a pitcher would stand on the mound and the ball would arch over his head, says Lloyd Young. That allowed the opposition to run wild. "But when we got Nels," Young says, "our pitchers never knew enough to step off the mound."

Al Young recalls that Ike Seaman was one such accidental victim, struck in the back by a Deveau peg. "Ike went down—it brought him down to his knees—and I went over and I said, 'Ike, for Christsakes, get out of the way!' He looked up at me and said, 'I will after this.'"

Off the field, Deveau considered himself a ladies' man, teammates recall.

"He and I roomed together," says Thorborne, "and I would be sound asleep, and he would bring these good-lookin' girls in to meet me. He had an awful line.

"On the way up to play ball in New Brunswick, we were in Springhill and stopped in a restaurant. So he asked to have the car— he never had a licence—and went off to see some friends because, at one time, he played ball up that way. So he was gone ... and gone ... and gone. So finally he drives up, and we say, 'We're going to be late!' And this girl beside him says to him, 'Why do you let them talk to you like that? It's your car!' His car? Jesus Christ, the man never owned a pack of cigarettes. But he was fillin' these women full."

Thorborne recalls another tale revolving around females, in which three or four Larrupers were caught with some women when the husband of one of them came home. "They all ran out of there without their overcoats, and they never even went back and got 'em."

Several years later, Zoomie Deveau would marry. The day after his nuptials he bumped into a couple of teammates at the Liverpool post office.

"Zoomie, I hear you got married last night," one of them began. "What happened?"

Deveau cast a wry grin. "I got up in the morning, I grabbed a hold of my pants, and I stared at the wife and I said, 'Here, wear them.'

'They won't fit me,' she said.

'Never forget that,' I said."

It was a manifestation of Deveau's intractable machismo that tainted the aftermath of Liverpool's first provincial title. Thorborne recounts that after they won the Nova Scotia championship in Halifax, Deveau jumped into a big car with a fellow near the ball diamond. Within moments, Deveau drove the car right into a streetcar. A Larrupers fan who had witnessed the accident shepherded Deveau into another car and drove him directly home to

Liverpool. "Never changed his clothes or anything," says Thorborne. "[The fan] called one of our executives—they were all big shots in town, they owned stores, they were lovely people—and they went and arranged everything. They hushed it up. I remember down at the hotel [in Halifax], we didn't know what to do. We had to hire a lawyer and it cost us $25. That was an awful night. After us winnin', it took the wind right out of our sails."

◆　◆　◆　◆

The Larrupers' 1938 Maritime senior baseball final against the St. Stephen St. Croixs had been a decade in the making, and in Liverpool it monopolized energies and kidnapped conversation. It was an event.

St. Stephen, on the other hand, was less enthusiastic. Can something be extraordinary for the eighth time? Here, at the end of this well-trod path of challengers, stood a new band of pretenders. A little younger than others, perhaps. Keener than most, too. But pretenders nonetheless. Still, this most professional of amateur teams would not take the Larrupers lightly. Nine years of programming and parades and pride made anything less than a full effort absolutely impossible.

Game one of the final in St. Stephen was postponed for three days because of rain. By the third rainout, players were bored and bitchy. "The sports writers are also getting jittery," wrote Ace Foley in the *Halifax Chronicle*. "It's too hot to sleep at night, and too warm to walk in the daylight.... If this keeps up much longer even the writers will quit."

However, game one was worth the wait. Liverpool's Laurie Thorborne and St. Stephen's Lefty Brownell battled for 11 innings, each surrendering just one run. In the bottom of the 12th inning, with no outs and two on, Ike Seaman came in without a warm-up, replacing Thorborne after the latter threw errantly to first baseman Lloyd Young.

"That St. Stephen ball field was like sand, and it was on the ball if you picked it up," reflects Thorborne. "Anyway, Lloyd had a tendency to have sore hands, and I always drove the ball to first, so this time I held back a little. It wasn't far off, but he stretched and tried to get it, instead of coming off the bag. It's the only error I ever made in my life. Ike went in and [on] the first pitch, bango!"

Shortstop Rainnie Moffatt singled home Harry (Dad) Boles with the winning run. Boles had scored St. Stephen's first run also. The final score was 2-1.

Liverpool evened the series the next day with a 4-2 win behind dipsy-doo artist Fred Kenney, who beat Ken Kallenberg. "The heavy-swinging Larrupers found Kallenberg greatly overrated," reported the *Halifax Herald*.

Nevertheless, Kallenberg was less of a disappointment than Baldy Moffatt was at first base. The *Herald* said that Moffatt had been playing first base "like a jittery grammar school kid, [and] attempted to tell umpire Ike Vanstone that [Larruper] Garneau Seaman had not touched first base. But though he threw his glove on the ground and raged around the infield like a prima donna he got nothing but a sharp no from the umpire and a barrage of boos from the St. Stephen fans."

In addition, Baldy nearly came to blows with Garneau Seaman and Danny Seaman. Garneau criticized Moffatt's fielding, and "it was necessary for the umpires to give them a lecture in etiquette," reported the *Herald*. "Later in the game Danny shoved Moffatt around when [Moffatt] insisted that Kenney continue to pitch with several balls that were damaged. Once more the arbiters were called in to quiet them."

Moffatt's exhibition embarrassed St. Stephen fans, who were long considered the Maritimes' most placid and most thoughtful. By 1938 the novelty of Moffatt had worn off, and he was no longer worth the 50 cents admission.

"Through the twelve innings of the opening game, Baldy was told when to order the hit and run ... the squeeze ... the double steal," said the *Herald*. "They [the fans] howled like wolves when he guessed wrong ... told him to turn in his uniform ... admit that old age had caught up with him. Once in the second game when they were riding him particularly hard, he crouched under an easy pop fly as if his life depended on it. The ball in his hand, he brandished it savagely at the derisive crowd."

The atmosphere in Liverpool was more genteel. Outfielder Al Young, five years a suffering Larruper, had been stricken suddenly with tonsillitis and could not make the trip to St. Stephen. "We had a policeman here, Bob White, and he came with his car, and my mother wrapped me up in some big quilts, and he put me in the back seat and we went downtown," Young says. "And at the time, there was a big telegraph office, and Larry Seldon's drug store had a big plate-glass window where they posted the scores. And I was sittin' there in the car like a little boy readin' them all off."

Larruper fans were as eclectic as those of any team in the region. "We were in St. Stephen and looked up in the grandstand and there'd be [this priest] sittin', watchin'," says Laurie Thorborne. "He was one of the best ball fans I ever knew, with us everywhere. But we had a lot of good fans. The executives used to hire two ... fellas to go over in the stands and holler, and you could hear them for two miles. [The executives] had some little words for them to say. Like, when Halifax was in town, they used to holler, 'You big city fellas and we small-town fellas, but we'll show ya.' And they got in shoutin' matches because we used to have quite a few fans up from Halifax. That's when they really got into it. It was terrible. Up and down the street at night after the ball game, it was terrible. Arguin', fightin'. Especially if we'd lose. This was the post-mortems on the ball games."

The Larrupers themselves proved congenial—if not crafty—hosts. "Liverpool threw a big party for us right before one of the games," recalls Jim Morell, "and the two teams went. I think the object was to get us drunk because they had beer and liquor and everything. They had cases and cases and cases of beer. And these fellas were all into it. But not many people on the St. Stephen team took even a drink, so the whole thing backfired."

For the town that longed, and the more than 2,000 fans who watched, game three of the 1938 Maritime finals was baffling. St. Stephen pummelled the Larrupers 6-0 behind Brownell's eight-hitter and Baldy Moffatt's two-run homer.

The next day, Liverpool evened the series at two games each with an 8-1 thrashing of Jim Morell. Danny Seaman homered, while Thorborne held the St. Croixs to six hits. Two of those were by Gordon Coffey, who, on that afternoon, became distracted by more than the score.

Between innings in game four, while chatting in the outfield with second baseman Sweet Pea McCarroll, Coffey noticed in the wall of faces ... a brown-haired beauty in the bleachers.

Coffey interrupted McCarroll and nodded at the stands. "Up there, that girl up there," he said with a thoughtful pause, "I'm going to marry her."

Thunderstruck by this abrupt announcement, but knowing that Coffey was not prone to reckless proclamations, McCarroll nodded and walked away quietly, more than a little mystified.

"That night," says Coffey, "we were out on the street and two or three of us players went up, and we were looking in on this dance. And these same girls—I later found out that they were friends and travelled around together—they were standing there looking on, too. Then this fellow introduced us to the three girls. That's when we first met. She used to have lunch with her sister living in Liverpool, and the next day, another fellow and I were out sitting on the steps, and who should come walking up the street again but this girl that I met at the dance the night before. So I hiked right down off the steps and I made the appointment right then to see her after the game."

A few months later the beauty married the ballplayer, and so began an endless happy ending for Gertrude Forbes and Gordon Coffey in a union that would outlast one world war and at least eight prime ministers.

◆ ◆ ◆ ◆

The crushing defeat in game four frustrated all of the St. Croixs, especially catcher Charlie Godfrey, the rotund cabbie who erupted when a force-out call at home plate went against the team. "Godfrey stepped towards the pitcher just after taking the throw and it was a few seconds before he realized how the decision had gone ... Enraged when umpire Ike Vanstone called a close decision against the St. Croixs, he threw the ball savagely to the ground ... and followed it with his mitt," reported the *Courier*. Added Alex Nickerson in the *Halifax Herald*, "Raging mightily [Godfrey] ... stalked out to the centre of the diamond. While he was storming around, Liverpool was running the bases like men possessed."

The jeers of Liverpool fans lashed at Godfrey as he stormed to the St. Stephen bench, where, in a crimson fury, Moffatt waited.

"You'll *never* catch for me again!" Moffatt screamed at Godfrey, unleashing a fresh wave of razzing from the Liverpool audience.

Godfrey slouched on the bench as Lloyd Kelly, fresh-faced and eager at age 21, trotted in to catch the rest of the game. The banishment was short-lived, however.

With the Maritime championship in the balance, the scheduled starter for game five—winner of games one and three—issued his coach an ultimatum. Said Lefty Brownell: "If Godfrey doesn't catch, I don't pitch."

Moffatt, ever the pragmatist, acquiesced. Godfrey returned to the line-up.

Liverpool was aglow for the showdown contest, and talk centred on the pending doom for Brownell, who was starting with just one day's rest instead of the customary three.

"If they send in Specs Brownell," wrote Ace Foley, "he'll get pasted ... because it is too much to expect of a man after [game three's] performance."

Initially, it had been Ken Kallenberg's game to start.

Brownell recalls Baldy Moffatt telling him after game three that he could whoop it up if he wanted. "So I went out on the town with Garneau Seaman, and I spent some time there at the Seamans' store. When I got back to the hotel, there was Baldy and Len Webber and two more there, and I could tell they had their heads together."

Moffatt called Brownell over. "We've been discussing things and here's what we've decided. Tomorrow, we're going to warm up the right-handers [Kallenberg and Morell] and we want you to go out and warm up, too. But don't warm up too hard, don't give them the impression that you're goin' in, don't answer any questions. Before we announce the line-ups and the battery, I'll talk to ya some."

On game day Moffatt approached Brownell on the sidelines and asked *the* question. The arm is good, answered Brownell. Fine, said Moffatt, go in.

"When they announced the battery—Brownell and Godfrey—cripes, you shoulda heard the crowd. 'We'll pound him,' they said," Brownell remembers with a smile.

It was soon apparent, however, that on this day the Liverpool Larrupers would not pound Brownell. He blanked Liverpool in the first two innings, allowed a run in the third, then eased through innings four, five and six. His curve broke, his fastball popped, his control was rarely better. But the Larrupers' Fred Kenney was also superb, and with Kenney's dipsy-doo ball working, Liverpool led 1-0 after six.

Then, nine outs from defeat, the St. Croixs went to work. Leading off the seventh, Art Lowe was nicked by a pitch and was awarded first base. Phil McCarroll then bunted safely, placing runners on first and second. Next up was Gordon Coffey.

"You want me to bunt?" Coffey asked Moffatt before stepping in.

Moffatt considered the options briefly, but the feisty tutor was not about to play for a tie. "Hit away," he said.

Kenney "was curving the outside corner on me," says Coffey. "I said that if he was going to throw me another one on the outside corner, I'll try it. I had a 36-inch bat, so I knew I could get it. And then I saw this outside pitch comin' in."

Coffey swung.

The ball ricocheted off the ozone and stopped rolling at the fence. Both runners scored, and Coffey pulled up at third. St. Stephen led 2-1.

Pitcher Laurie Thorborne, who was warming up on the sidelines, still winces when he recalls the critical blow. As Coffey was walking to the batter's box, "I went out to the mound, and I said, 'For heaven's sake, Freddie, don't throw him an outside ball. If you do, we're done. Walk 'em.' On my way back to the dugout, I heard *bang* and I looked out and I saw Danny Seaman running after the ball ... Freddie had no head at all."

Coffey eventually scored to make it 3-1, and Liverpool scored once in their half of the seventh, but stalled thereafter. The St. Croixs added two more in the ninth as Brownell completed a 5-2, five-hit masterpiece, striking out nine for his third win in the series and his second win in three days. St. Stephen had its seventh Maritime title in eight years.

For the Larrupers, the top of the mountain was made of quicksand. They had come close—three innings close—and the stands were sullen in the immediate aftermath.

After a few moments had passed and the St. Croixs had gushed just a bit, a Larruper walked across the field and clasped Brownell's hand in congratulations.

"Next year," said Laurie Thorborne.

◆ 1 9 3 9 ◆
THE END
OF THE LINE

"I think they must've won somethin'."
—Lloyd Kelly—

O N A GENTLE AUGUST EVENING following a ball game
in Woodland, Maine, Sweet Pea McCarroll walked slowly
into his room carrying a new suitcase—a gift from his
teammates. A few moments passed before he began to peel off his
uniform. What was usually a quick change, on this night was a
deliberate, reverential ceremony. First the cap, then the sweater,
then the pants, and so it went, until all of the components lay flat
on the floor, his worn-smooth second baseman's glove at the head.
Then McCarroll stepped back and gazed upon the remnants of his
youth.

That evening, Sweet Pea became Phil, and the next day he
boarded the train for North Dartmouth, Massachusetts, to enter
the novitiate at Holy Cross to study for the priesthood. "The day
had to come when he would settle upon a profession," said the
Saint Croix Courier, "but it is a surprise even to those who know
him best that he would settle down to that extent." (McCarroll
eventually decided against the priesthood.)

An equally significant loss to the St. Croixs was pitcher Ken
Kallenberg, who, like McCarroll, boarded a train in the summer of
1939. He, too, had gotten the call.

◆　◆　◆　◆

Like many adolescents growing up in the St. Croix Valley in the
1930s, Kallenberg was an athlete by default.

"When I was a kid the only thing we had to do was swim. We
didn't have any swimming pools in town, so we'd walk down 10
miles to Red Beach in the morning, swim all day, then walk back.
One place would be quite narrow, and a bunch of us from Calais
would be on one bank, and a bunch from St. Stephen would be on
the other bank. We'd get yelling back and forth, and then one of us

would yell, 'Fuck the queen,' and they'd be jumpin' in the water to get us. When they'd get across the river, if there were too many, we'd take off. If there was only one or two, we'd go meet 'em, then they'd turn around and go back."

Americans against Canadians, Protestants against Catholics, neighborhood against neighborhood. These shifting allegiances collided for pick-up ball games on sprawling fields with cow flaps for bases and an unravelling sphere for a ball. Here, formal instruction was an impractical luxury, and natural ability prevailed. And Ken Kallenberg was a natural.

At his first high school track meet he tied for first in the high jump, placed third in the javelin and won the shot put, even though he had first held an official shot just one week earlier. He also pitched for the high school baseball team.

Although coiled tightly inside, Kallenberg appeared bothered by nothing. His speech was slow, his gait was casual, and relaxation was both his sacrament and his armor. The demeanor puzzled many but annoyed few, because Kallenberg was polite, generous and a hell of a ballplayer.

Recalls Jim Morell: "Ken would say, 'Let's go over to Calais,' and he'd go in, put 25 cents in the record player, and go out and get a cone of ice cream or milk shake and leave the record player going. He'd put money in and never stayed to listen to anything. He'd go over and buy a shirt and a pair of shoes, and have $15 spent before he'd go down the street. The next day he'd be goin' around, 'Wanna buy a pair of shoes? I'll sell 'em to ya for five bucks.' He'd be broke. He'd do anything to spend money. If he had nothing else to do, he'd go out and get a haircut."

Kallenberg's father regularly fired off clippings extolling Ken's baseball accomplishments to the *Boston Globe*'s well-connected sports columnist, Billy Cunningham, who, in turn, forwarded them to the Boston Red Sox of the American League. The correspondence paid off handsomely. In 1936 the Red Sox and the Boston Bees (formerly the Braves) invited Kallenberg to attend morning practices in Boston. Not yet 18, Kenny declined both invitations.

Before the 1937 season, Kallenberg's father, Arthur, received a letter from Billy Evans, the Red Sox's chief scout of the minor leagues. (Kallenberg was still a minor, and he needed parental consent for contracts.) Evans requested that Ken report with 50 other prospects to a training camp in Little Rock, Arkansas, operated by managers of Red Sox minor league teams. This offer was accepted. He and six others from that camp were subsequently assigned to a team in Moultrie, Georgia, in a lowly professional circuit called the Georgia-Florida League.

In Moultrie, Kallenberg's sore throwing arm hampered his performance, so he returned to St. Stephen in mid-summer and helped the St. Croixs win the 1937 Maritime senior baseball championship.

In May 1938, the prodigy quietly boarded the train to Boston for another shot with the Red Sox. Now the venerable club—the choice of the Maritimes—began to take him seriously. They worked on his delivery and his fielding, and insisted that his curve ball improve. When the team was out of town, Kallenberg was tutored at Fenway Park by an affable and patient Irishman named Hugh Duffy, one of the last major league players to hit .400 in one season. In addition, the Red Sox assigned Kallenberg to the St. Augustine club in the developmental Boston Park League.

"This park league was set up all over Boston," says Kallenberg, "spread all over the god-damned place. I'd go for a workout in the morning under Duffy, and he'd give me a handful of bus tokens for the subway and tell me to go [to] some god-damned place I never even heard of. I'd pitch a ball game and play the outfield. Then I'd find my way back to the place that I was staying. Then, a couple of days later, he'd give me some bus tokens and tell me to go someplace else, maybe with an entirely different team. Some of his outfielders he would send one place, some to another place. He'd have them goin' all the time, playin' ball. There'd be a nucleus for a team, but he'd send new people in all the time."

Although not chummy with them, Kallenberg became at least comfortable around major leaguers. Mostly, though, he kept his mouth shut and ears open and watched the icons tumble. Particularly resonant was the fall of former American League MVP Robert Moses (Lefty) Grove.

"Lefty Grove was loud, uncouth," Kallenberg says of the Hall of Famer. "From the first time I saw him and listened to him talk, he was all bluff. He was drawin' his money, and I don't think he gave a god damn if he won a ball game or not. It was just his attitude. He was "The Greatest." Not only that, but it was the type of language that he used and the things that he talked about. Stuff that I wasn't used to. I can swear—and I heard swearin' in the service—but that stuff comin' out of him was a different type of profanity. Everything he said was profane."

Nor was Kallenberg fond of Ben Chapman, a 29-year-old outfielder from Nashville, Tennessee, who hit .340 in 1938, the second-best average on the team. Kallenberg encountered Chapman during morning batting practice.

"[Coach] Tone Dailey was feeding me balls out of a mail bag in the back of the mound. It was one of the first times I pitched batting practice. Chapman came up, and he began whistling them right back through the mound. So Dailey said, 'You know why he's doing that? He's getting it right square over the plate. There ain't no other place for the ball to go other than straight back.' He tossed me another ball. 'Next pitch you throw, throw right at his god-damned head, loosen him up. You'll find he'll begin to hit them to one side or the other.' So the next pitch I threw, it was right at his head. Chapman just got out of the way of it. Then I threw another one in there, and it came right back through the middle again. Dailey said, 'Throw at his god-damned head!' So I reared back and let it go and got him right between the shoulder blades. He came out with the bat, and I thought he was gonna throw it at me and or club me with it. Dailey said, 'Don't pay any attention to him, he's nothin' but a prick, anyway.'

"I found that those guys were just as human as anyone else. They are alcoholics and everything else. [But] you realized there was a difference between professional and amateur baseball. The baseball [with the St. Croixs] was only played for a sport, only played a couple of times a week. If you are going to play professional ball—even down in the low minor leagues—you had to want it so god-damned bad that you'll fight to get it. That's the single thing that you have to have on your mind. And you gotta take coaching."

Kallenberg's first game in the Boston Park League was a 10-3 victory. He struck out five, walked two and gave up seven hits, all singles. He also doubled and singled. In four other starts, he lost just once.

However, after eight weeks in the big city, the good times ended.

Pitching batting practice one day, Kallenberg caught his spikes in the canvas that was always placed over the pitcher's mound during practice. He tore some muscles in his side. "So I went home for 13 days [in July], and when I came back my arm went all to hell. So they released me." Kallenberg says he was disappointed but not surprised.

He returned to Calais, where a doctor extracted bone chips from his right arm and admonished that it needed a full year's rest. Despite the warning, Kallenberg was on the St. Stephen diamond again in a few weeks, helping the St. Croixs to another Maritime championship.

In 1939, as the world headed for war, Kenny Kallenberg headed south for a final shot at the great American dream. Bill Terry, general manager of the New York Giants of the National League, signed him to play for Milford, Delaware, in the Eastern Shore League. The condition was that if his arm recovered fully, he would climb to a higher level next season.

The Eastern Shore League was an eight-team, Class D teaching circuit whose teams played the same number of games as major league teams did—154, most of them under the lights. Teams were owned by major league clubs, which supplied uniforms previously worn by the eminences above. In Delaware, Kallenberg won nine and lost four with "Carl Hubbell," his idol, stitched into his jersey. His arm ached again, however, and his performance dropped sharply.

Thus in 1940 it was back to Milford, where his 18-7 record proved that he and his afflicted limb were finally ready for faster company.

However, before what should have been Kallenberg's pinnacle year—1941—Bill Terry wrote him and asked what his military draft number was. Kallenberg cringed. The number was very low, indicating that he could be an early draftee. Learning this, the Giants, who the year before had penciled him in for spring training, offered Kallenberg another minor league contract. Upset, the pitcher reasoned that if they were going to relegate him to the baseball hinterlands, at least he would make the mighty New York Giants pay for his services.

"There was a certain rule about how much you could be paid in those leagues. In Milford it was $100 a month, but there were ways of getting around it. From the parent club you'd always be getting extra money, but you'd get it in cash. You'd have nothin' to show it. That's how they'd stay within the rules. The higher the league, the more they would pay. I was getting $300 to $500 extra a month from the New York Giants, and a few times in Delaware they'd pass the hat. The most I got from that was $70. Or, they'd come around and tell you to come down to the store the next day and pick out a pair of shoes."

Kallenberg mulled it over, then responded. "I wrote back and told them all right, but I wanted more money. Well, I got the same contract back in the envelope. I sent it back to them and said not to send it again, or I'd go in the service anyway. I got it back again, and I stuck it right back in an envelope. That afternoon I volunteered for the draft."

◆ ◆ ◆ ◆

The final season began sluggishly for the St. Croixs. Their exhibition schedule lagged several weeks behind that of other teams, and when it finally commenced, they lost their first three games, including one to the Calais Blue Sox when coach Moffatt spitefully inserted himself as pitcher.

An ugly start for the area's premier sports team was at least appropriate in the summer of 1939, as the cant of greater conflict vibrated through the St. Croix Valley.

A guard of ex-servicemen warily circled St. Stephen's water supply at Maxwell Crossing, where new lights cast a leery spotlight. Equipment normally found in the armory was hauled furtively to a secret location. Four members of the fire department were called into the militia. And when the Red Cross summoned volunteers for a disaster relief committee, town hall overflowed with the earnest, the concerned and the uncertain.

"Look for a moment at these leaders," lectured the *Saint Croix Courier* a few months before Canada declared war on Germany. "Hitler himself, a case for mental experts, fanatically devoted to obscure dreams of greatness, a rabble-rouser whose frenzy and violence are keys to an unbalanced mind, and whose appearance and deportment would in less tragic circumstances fit well into a comic opera. Field Marshall Goering, a pilot in the World War ... a killer if there ever was one ... preferring to maneuver into a position where he had his guns at his enemy's back and then blasting away without pause or let-up.... And Joseph Goebbels, propaganda chief, the most unpopular man in Germany, imbued with all the hatred of normal persons, physically maimed as he is, an apostle of vice and perfidy whose diabolically clever mind has twisted German thought into channels far from the truth but very useful for the purposes of National Socialism. These are Germany's leaders— vicious, unprincipled, barbarian fanatics. At their door will lay the blame for whatever may occur as a result of Germany's continuing conquests."

Overseas malfeasance had supplanted amateur baseball as St. Stephen's prime summer concern. No matter, the team had plenty of pride to sustain one more drive, a final thrust to "please the fans and place his home team as a winner on the sporting map," as Bill Whitlock had preached at the decade's onset.

Some key players had left the team, but several remained. Lefty Brownell was easily the best pitcher in the Maritimes, Gordon Coffey was its premier outfielder, and veteran Rainnie Moffatt was likely one of the most tenacious shortstops in the country. Baldy Moffatt doubled as coach and first baseman, the former clearly his strength.

As well, the organization was solid. Len Webber was elected president of the New Brunswick Amateur Baseball Association, but still served as team secretary. The regular duties were left to manager Arlo Hayman, a cautious and hardworking volunteer. Another constant was the team's selection of umpire for playoff games, 28-year-old Johnny Lifford.

Few disputed the calls of umpire Johnny Lifford. During a boxing career spanning 20 years and 235 amateur and professional bouts, he charged opponents with a savage two-fisted attack that made him one of the region's most popular athletes. He was never knocked out.

The dark-haired, pallid-faced pugilist with baby-doll eyes and a passion for buttermilk was the lightweight, welterweight and middleweight champion of the Maritimes.

In June 1939 Lifford shifted his fighting base from Saint John to St. Stephen, where he earned a few dollars umpiring senior ball games and travelling to Cape Breton periodically to handle games in the semi-professional Colliery League.

"He's the only umpire who came near throwing me out of a game," recalls Gordon Coffey. "He was umpiring one of the bases and he called me out. It was a high tag, and I argued pretty forcefully. Finally, I got mad and said, 'No wonder you can't fight. You can't see!' He said, 'If you want to finish this game, you'd better get over to the bench and shut up.' I shut up."

No angel of etiquette, Lifford did nasty things under the influence of hooch. One year as the ferry carrying teams across the Bay of Fundy was docking, Lifford dashed off ahead of the teams. Brandishing a long, pointed knife he called his "toad stabber," the inebriated boxer clutched the ballplayers' neckties and slashed them at the knot as the victims stood paralysed, smiles of consternation on their faces. The only free passage Lifford granted was to an Anglican minister and his collar.

On it went, as Lifford's treasure-trove of truncated ties soon bulged his pockets, and his laughter became increasingly maniacal. After several minutes of this, St. Stephen catcher Theo (Muddy) McLain—feeling he could take no more of Lifford's dangerous tomfoolery—removed his jacket.

"C-c-c-c'mon," screamed McLain, his fists high in a fighter's stance. "Put down the knife and c-c-c-c-c'mon."

Some teammates leapt towards McLain and attempted to muffle his challenge before Lifford noticed. It was too late. Lifford looked back and grinned at the burly backstop.

"Look, Theo," said Lifford, beginning his lesson in a calmly sinister voice. "You are a ballplayer, right?"

McLain said nothing, but at least he had stopped struggling to break free of his teammates.

"And Theo," continued the middleweight champion of the Maritimes in a still calmer voice, "I am a fighter, right? That's my game, right?"

McLain said something about upsetting the team and that Lifford ought to pay for it. The boxer's bald logic, however, seemed to sift through. So after a few seconds of thought, McLain dropped his gutsy challenge, and Lifford dropped his toad stabber, and everyone walked off with their erect, little stubby ties pointing the way.

◆ ◆ ◆ ◆

Whatever the quality of the opponent, time was the St. Croixs' most potent foe, blunting the team's sharp edge and permitting complacency to seep in. As the St. Croixs began their most arduous playoff year, could artifice compensate for age?

In the opening game of the best-of-five New Brunswick prelimi-
nary series, the answer appeared to be no.

In St. Stephen, Fredericton-Devon southpaw Jimmy Vandestine
beat the St. Croixs 6-3. Part way through the contest, Baldy
Moffatt—his testiness now embedded in the team psyche—pulled
the St. Croixs from the field, insisting that Vandestine was balking.
As his players sat passively on the bench, he began conspicuously
stuffing bats into a duffel bag. Once again his players cringed, but
Moffatt continued to scoop up the bats.

"Baldy," whispered Coffey, "you can't get away with this."

Moffatt lowered his head. "I know. But we're scaring the hell out
of 'em."

Having made his point, Moffatt eventually ordered the St.
Croixs to return. Nevertheless, it remained a desperate measure by
a coach who knew his was no longer a superior team. "Is it possible
that St. Stephen is going to be knocked off in the first round of the
New Brunswick senior playdowns?" asked the *Telegraph-Journal*.

That very possibility increased significantly when, on a St.
Stephen construction site, sloppily piled bricks fell from a hod on
the second floor and struck St. Croixs pitcher Brownell on the head
and shoulder. An ambulance rushed him to Chipman Memorial
Hospital, where, dizzy and in pain, he was examined and released.
In less than a week Brownell would recover fully.

The Fredericton-Devon team was less fortunate. A car returning
several players home from game one during the wee hours skidded
in heavy gravel, struck a concrete bridge abutment, rolled in the
ditch and burst into flames. Everyone survived. Most of the
occupants crawled out, but playing coach Bill Lifford was pulled
from the car just seconds before the gas tank exploded. Among the
escapees was star pitcher Jimmy Vandestine, a major league prospect. The accident clearly unnerved the team because the St. Croixs
went on to win the next three games and the series.

The provincial quarter-finals began as St. Stephen and the Minto
Miners split the first two games. The third was thus the pivotal
game, and it was a 13-inning classic that featured herculean relief
by the St. Croixs' Don Norton—sometime pinch runner, sometime
right fielder, sometime third baseman, but always the Golden Boy.

By the late 1930s Donald Norton was an elite athlete living a
charmed existence. At one track meet he tied the New Brunswick

high school record for the 220-yard dash (24 seconds) and set new marks in the standing broad jump (21 feet, two inches) and 100-yard dash (10 2/5 seconds). With his elongated neck, sloping shoulders and legs so thick that they seemed to belong to a larger physique, Norton had the sleek frame of the very swift. He was also a skilled skier and tennis player, and was a football stand-out.

Although no sport seemed beyond his mastery, he remained humble. "He didn't try to be the big shot," says Jim Morell. "He just played it easy and therefore got along with everybody." Norton was also faultlessly deferential to his parents' wishes, including their request that he not play baseball on Sundays. "He wasn't the type of boy who thought he knew more than his parents did," his mother noted many years later.

Norton graduated second in a class of 14 at Milltown High School. At Mount Allison University in Sackville, New Brunswick, students nicknamed him Whizzer and elected him student union president. There, he assaulted intercollegiate track and field records and dominated most meets with a pure, virile athleticism. In the early 1940s he beat Canadian sprint champion Peter Taylor in the 100-yard dash in St. Catharines, Ontario. The victory received little attention, but for Whizzer Norton it proved a point.

His most heroic act was not competitive, however. On the night of December 16, 1941, as flames roared through a Mount Allison men's residence, Norton tore from floor to floor and roused sleeping students, shouting instructions on how to improvise ropes from bed sheets. As flames closed in, Norton decided that he could do no more and he leapt from a third-storey window into a fireman's net. The fire killed four people. Norton had saved at least a dozen lives.

In 1942, immediately after graduating with his bachelor of science degree, he enlisted in the Royal Canadian Air Force. The fastest runner in a Canadian military uniform received his wings in 1943.

During his training in the RCAF, Norton escaped serious injury one night in January 1944. As a half moon peeked through a persistent cloud cover, he and four others survived when their Whitley V exploded during a practice takeoff near the Honeybourne airfield in Worcester County, England. Wrote the wing commander in the accident report: "At 100 ft. over the edge of the aerodrome the port engine cut dead, following a bang and a cloud of sparks. This pupil pilot endeavored to gain height flying straight ahead, but was unable to maintain height. At 20:37 he crashed into a field, hit some trees and caught fire."

Still conscious, Norton was rushed to hospital with a fractured right clavicle. His right leg required some stitches, but otherwise, said the confidential hospital report, "recovery uneventful."

Fourteen days later he was back in the navigator's chair.

In March of the same year, the handsome, young navigator wed a beautiful Torontonian named Sally Bircher. Their union seemed ideal and destined. The wedding choir sang O Perfect Love.

A few months later, at 1 a.m. on June 8, the *Halifax III* carrying St. Stephen's Golden Boy and eight others was shot down in battle in a field adjacent to a farm in Ronchois, France. "Fire was ... on board before the crash," said a report not filed until August 1946, "and the bodies of the occupants were badly burned and disintegrated as the aircraft exploded upon crashing ... The aircraft had buried itself very deeply and must have burnt for hours."

Flying Officer Donald Norton—J-26934, 420 Squadron RCAF—was laid to rest in Row D, Grave No. 6, in Poix de la Somme Churchyard, near Amiens, France. He was three weeks shy of age 23.

◆ ◆ ◆ ◆

For the St. Croixs, game three of the New Brunswick quarter-finals against the Minto Miners was a disaster. Down 8-1 after just four innings, playing-coach Baldy Moffatt concluded that the game was out of reach and called young third baseman Donald Norton over to the mound. In a poorly veiled act of surrender, Moffatt slapped the ball into Norton's glove, all the while hoping that the team could regroup tomorrow, no matter how unwieldy the score grew in this game.

Good luck, Moffatt told Norton, and trotted back over to first base.

Suddenly St. Stephen's bats awoke. By the end of the fifth the St. Croixs had cut the gap to 8-7, and they pulled even shortly thereafter when Norton tripled home shortstop Rainnie Moffatt. In the meantime, Norton continued to mow down the Miners as his mates welcomed an old friend—resourcefulness.

"During the two-hour struggle," reported the Fredericton

Gleaner, "the pew-holders were treated to all the thrills including ... the odd hidden ball trick which 'Baldy' Moffatt pulled out of moth balls to catch Boyce and Thompson flat-footed at first and stop the Miners' threats."

Tied 8-8 after nine innings, the teams traded zeros in the 10th, 11th and 12th. Norton showed no signs of faltering even through by the top of the 13th—his ninth inning on the mound—he had permitted just two hits, both of them feeble. Finally, in the bottom of the 13th more than four hours after the first pitch, Rainnie Moffatt doubled, then scored the winning run on an error. St. Stephen now led the series 2-1 and would go on to win the provincial quarter-final in five games.

After sweeping past Plaster Rock in straight games, the St. Croixs clashed with the Saint Johns in the provincial final. With adequate power, good pitching and outstanding defence, the Saint Johns that year had thrice taken the measure of the barnstorming House of David, who in turn proclaimed them the best team they had ever faced in the Maritimes.

True to predictions, the Saint Johns beat the St. Croixs two of the first three games. They returned home as the first Saint John team in a decade to flirt seriously with the New Brunswick baseball championship. The city salivated. "Those fans who wait for the playoffs here's the best chance they ever had to get in on the kill," wrote H. J. Osborne in the *Telegraph-Journal.*

More than 2,000 spectators crowded into Shamrock Park to wish ill of their native son Lefty Brownell. Once more, however, the bespectacled southpaw punished the city that, five years before, had treated him with indifference and ingratitude. He won 5-0 as the Saint Johns committed seven errors.

"It was the worst display of baseball a home team has dished out to the home fans in years," blasted Osborne, who reasoned that nervousness had hindered the local team. Still, he concluded, the Saint Johns were simply outwitted. "'Baldy' Moffatt ... pulled some smart stuff on Saturday and it was due to his headwork that the Saint Johns blew up.... His knowledge of how a team can get the most out of a game had brought the St. Croixs through on more than one occasion."

The Saint Croixs went on to win the deciding game in St. Stephen 4-2 for their ninth consecutive provincial championship.

But it was only the second provincial title for the group of young athletes who had joined the team one year before: Charlie Weatherby, Dana Miles, Cliff Middlemiss, Lloyd Kelly.

For Lloyd Kelly, the catcher, No. 7, the baseball playoffs provided a welcome counterbalance for Lloyd Kelly, the infantryman, No. G17302.

On September 1, 1939, in the middle of the Minto series, 22-year-old Kelly enlisted. Baseball, he reasoned, had to be sacrificed—or did it? If only there was some way to attend basic training in Woodstock, New Brunswick, and play ball, too.

Kelly spoke to his quartermaster in Woodstock, who just happened to be named Len Webber and who said he would see what he could do. Webber knew Kelly well, and as a former team manager, he knew the St. Croixs even better.

Webber spoke to the colonel, who just happened to be named Ganong—H. N. Ganong, a relative of St. Stephen's first family of chocolate. After less than a week of basic training, Private Kelly had permission to return to battle on the baseball diamond for the duration of the playoffs.

◆ ◆ ◆ ◆

In Nova Scotia, the Liverpool Larrupers breezed to their second straight provincial title. The team that had pushed the Saint Croixs to the limit in last year's Maritime final were stronger still in 1939. Whereas only two Larrupers hit better than .300 in the previous Nova Scotia playdowns, in 1939 five had broken that barrier with a team average of .296—more than 50 points better than last year. (By comparison, the St. Croixs hit a woeful .149 in the 1939 New Brunswick playdowns, with only Coffey batting above .300.)

The biggest improvement, though, was in Liverpool's pitching. By acquiring left-handed sensation Jim (Schoolboy) Mont from Halifax, the Larrupers had almost rendered the regular season superfluous and had turned the Nova Scotia playdowns into a foregone conclusion.

Good-looking, young and talented, Mont was working in the mail room at Simpson's department store in Halifax when the Larrupers promised him $25 a week—under the table—plus a job with the Mersey paper company. So the baby-faced, university-educated extrovert packed his bags. He was 23 years old.

"I never did see the $25 a week," he says, "but I never bothered going after it. I had a tremendous time down there."

Fringe benefits compensated. "There are a lot of good waves out at Summerville Beach [outside Liverpool] in the summertime. And mister, you can get out there in those waves with a pretty girl, and get far enough out so no one can see ya, and...."

One of 11 children of a Halifax coal company manager, Mont was one of four husbands of a Liverpool woman not known to strictly adhere to marriage vows. Friends say that the bad marriage gnawed at the young man, who turned to the bottle for solace. About the only thing more unorthodox than Mont's marital life was his pitching motion.

In Halifax, coach Steamer Lucas, a veteran of the Toronto Maple Leafs of the International Baseball League who used to come to the ball park dressed in a suit, insisted that Mont use an elaborate wind-up that even the pitcher thought bizarre. Still, Mont obeyed.

"He had this way of pitchin', like kickin' a light bulb out of the ceiling," says Al Young, of the Liverpool Larrupers. "He seemed off balance every time he pitched." Recalls Liverpool journalist Armond Wigglesworth: "I think that he wasted most of his energy in that kick. He kicked as high as anyone I've ever seen. It was effective for a while because you wouldn't know where the ball was coming from, but you can steal on a high kicker, too. It was the goddamnest thing I've ever seen."

◆　◆　◆　◆

The Larrupers were heavy favorites in the final, especially in the Nova Scotian press. Alex Nickerson, of the *Halifax Herald*, wrote that St. Stephen had seen better days. "Their painful struggle through the New Brunswick playdowns indicates that the end of the trail is near for several performers who helped make Maritime baseball history in the last decade."

After game one such observations appeared reasonable. The Larrupers pounded St. Stephen ace Brownell 11-2, their first defeat of the southpaw who had beaten them three times the year before.

However, in less than 20 hours, Brownell returned.

Relieving starter Don Norton in the fifth when St. Stephen trailed 3-1, he stifled Liverpool on two hits while teammates chipped away at the lead. Aided by Liverpool's five errors, the St. Croixs jumped ahead and stayed there, winning 5-3 and using a little "inside baseball" in the pinch.

In the ninth, the Larrupers had Vic Winters on second and Nelson Deveau coming to bat. "Making a pretense of trying to catch Winters off the base, shortstop Rainnie Moffatt sprinted to second, Winters followed then when the shortstop raced back to his position, the big Liverpool slugger stepped a few paces off the bag. It was fatal. Unnoticed by Winters second baseman [Dana] Miles had sneaked up to the bag, a lightning throw from Brownell, who had the play timed perfectly, caught Winters flat-footed," described Nickerson in the *Halifax Herald*.

The St. Croixs—powered it seemed by loyalty to their own legend—had tied a series many had originally deemed a mismatch.

More surprising yet, the St. Croixs and Brownell won the third game 5-4, moving them within a single victory of their eighth Maritime title in the decade. That game, however, was extraordinary for another reason—the weather. "[The game] finished up as a farce," wrote Jimmy Smith in the *Halifax Herald*, "with rain turning the diamond into a sea of mud and the fans pleading with umpire-in-chief Herb Dixon of Liverpool to call off hostilities. But the teams struggled through to the finish with players slipping around in the mire, and making championship ball practically an impossibility....

"Today's game should have been called in the fifth or as late as the sixth when the teams were tied four-all. A slight drizzle faced the teams when the game got under way and except for momentary lapses got worse at the tilt progressed. In the seventh and eighth heats, players as well as spectators were soaked but umpire Dixon permitted the game to continue, despite the fact that a great many of the thousand fans dashed for cover."

In game four, Liverpool's Thorborne bested St. Stephen's Morell, paving the way for perhaps the region's most important baseball game in a decade, and its most contrasting pitching match-up—Brownell versus Mont.

For Brownell, the pre-game routine was fixed from the time he threw his first pitch as a teenager back home in West Saint John. Proper sleep, a proper meal, longjohns and a long warm-up. It worked well for this most determined of pitchers.

For the free-spirited Mont, this night would bring on alien preparation, which is to say, any preparation at all. Soon after game four had ended, veteran Laurie Thorborne and catcher Nelson Deveau cornered Mont in a hotel room and insisted that, together, they go over every St. Stephen batter, discussing weaknesses, strengths and strategy. Keep the pitch low and outside, throw this guy tight, keep that guy loose. Over and over Thorborne and Deveau quizzed Mont until he had memorized each batter's profile. Then they started from the top and worked through the line-up again.

In the end all three agreed that the key man was centre fielder Gordon Coffey. To mute his bat was to nullify the St. Croixs' punch, and with Brownell going for the St. Croixs there seemed little room for error.

◆　◆　◆　◆

On a bright autumn afternoon more than 1,200 fans arrived at the St. Stephen ball park sensing that, no matter what the score, they would see something beautiful die.

The team of sportsmanship and intellect that over a span of 10 years and under three names helped define their community for all of the Maritimes would not play another ball game.

It was no secret that the St. Croixs were thinking of disbanding—the players were talking openly about it, says Coffey. The catalysts were the war and waning fan support. Perhaps victory had lost some of its edge in St. Stephen. Besides, a number of players had already traded ball uniforms for military ones. The Second World War would put an end to the team, but in the meantime, the Liverpool Larrupers would see to the rest.

Liverpool struck quickly, scoring three times in the first inning and setting the home team back on its heels. Mont, intensely nervous before the game, breezed through the first inning, aware that leading off the second inning would be the mighty Coffey.

As Coffey burrowed into the batter's box, Mont stood on the mound and took the deepest and longest breath of his life. For just this moment he had practised a bastard breaking ball—three fingers hooked around and under, and a nasty snap of the wrist upon release.

Coffey looked out, Mont kicked and fired. Strike one, looking.

Next pitch: strike two, looking.

Next pitch: strike three, looking.

"When I struck him out with that crazy ball of mine, I knew I was home free," says Mont. "I had him. No question about that. He never took the bat off his shoulder. Early in the game, when you get that feeling, 'I can beat this team,' there was no stoppin' us."

In the third inning Liverpool moved ahead 4-0, then put the game away with four more in the eighth. The final score was 8-1.

After the last out Mont raced to the Liverpool dugout and hugged Thorborne, screaming, "We did it! We did it! We did it!"

As the Larrupers danced about, young St. Stephen catcher Kelly walked over to Coffey, who stood calmly near first base surveying the celebration.

"I think they must've won somethin'," said Kelly.

Coffey smiled a little, politely, and turned away quietly.

Wasting little time, Kelly—who would be dressed in khaki the next day and headed for basic training—collected his mitt and exchanged his spikes for sneakers. With the spikes draped over his shoulders, he began the half-hour trek home on a dusty side road, a path where a young man could be alone with his thoughts.

"But baseball," he says, "wasn't on my mind."

BIBLIOGRAPHY

Published Material

Appel, Martin, and Burt Goldblatt. *Baseball's Best: The Hall of Fame Gallery.* New York: Macmillan Publishing Co. Inc., 1977.

Axelrod, Paul. "Moulding the Middle Class: Student Life at Dalhousie University in the 1930s." *Acadiensis: Journal of the History of the Atlantic Region.* XV, No. 1 (Autumn 1985).

Breault, Ann. *The Journey.* St. Stephen, N.B.: St. Croix Printing and Publishing Co. Ltd., 1977.

Campbell, D'Ann. *Women at War with America: Private Lives in a Patriotic Era.* Cambridge, Mass.: Harvard University Press, 1984.

Cauz, Louis. *Baseball's Back in Town.* Toronto: Controlled Media Corp. undated

Chafe, William Henry. *The American Woman: Her Changing Social, Economic, and Political Roles.* New York: Oxford University Press, 1976.

Colombo, John Robert. *Colombo's Canadian References.* Toronto: Oxford University Press, 1976.

Couzens, Gerald Secor. *A Baseball Album.* New York: Lippincott and Crowell, 1980.

Crossman, E. J. *Freshwater Fishes of Canada.* Ottawa: Government of Canada, 1973.

Degler, Carl N. *At Odds: Women and the Family in America from the Revolution to the Present.* New York: Oxford University Press, 1980.

Dickson, Paul. *The Dickson Baseball Dictionary.* New York: Facts on File, 1989.

Foley, Ace. *The First Fifty Years: The Life and Times of a Sportswriter.* Windsor, N. S.: Lancelot Press Limited, 1970.

Folster, David. *Elite: The New Brunswick Sports Hall of Fame.* Fredericton, N.B., 1983.

———. "The Old Home Team." *The Atlantic Advocate* (July 1968).

———. "The Sweet, Sweet Smell of Success." *Atlantic Insight* (February 1983).

Forbes, E. R. "Cutting the Pie into Smaller Pieces: Matching Grants and Relief in the Maritime Provinces during the 1930s." *Acadiensis: Journal of the History of the Atlantic Region,* XVVII, No. 1 (Autumn 1987).

Grant, B. J. *When Rum Was King.* Fredericton, N.B.: Fiddlehead Poetry Books and Goose Lane Editions, 1984.

Halberstam, David. *Summer of '49.* New York: William Morrow and Company, Inc., 1989.

Hamilton, William B. *The Macmillan Book of Canadian Place Names.* Toronto: Macmillan of Canadan, 1978.

Harper, John Russell. *The Historical Directory of New Brunswick Newspapers and Periodicals.* The University of New Brunswick, 1961.

Herstein, H. H., L. J. Hughes and R. C. Kirbyson. *Challenge and Survival: The History of Canada.* Scarborough: Prenctice-Hall of Canada, Ltd., 1970.

Hoch, Paul. *Rip Off the Big Game: The Exploitation of Sports by the Power Elite.* Garden City: Doubleday & Company, Inc., 1972.

Howell, Colin D. "Baseball, Class and Community in the Maritime Provinces, 1870-1910." *Social History* (November 1989).

Holway, John. *Voices from the Great Black Baseball Leagues.* New York: Dodd, Mead & Company, 1975.

Honig, Donald, and Lawrence Ritter. *The 100 Greatest Baseball Players of All Time.* New York: Crown Publishers, Inc., 1981.

————. *The National League: An Illustrated History.* New York: Crown Publishers, Inc., 1983.

Horn, Michiel, ed. *The Dirty Thirties: Canada in the Great Depression.* Toronto: The Copp Clark Publishing Company, 1972.

Humber, William. *Cheering for the Home Team: The Story of Baseball in Canada.* Erin, Ontario: The Boston Mills Press, 1983.

Kahn, Roger. *The Boys of Summer.* New York: Signet, 1971.

Kirschner, Allen. *Great Sports Reporting.* New York: Laurel Leaf Library, 1969.

Leacy, F. H. *Historical Statistics of Canada*, 2nd ed. Ottawa: Statistics Canada, 1983.

MacLeod, Sue. "Small Towns: St. Stephen, N.B." *Atlantic Insight* (March 1986).

Melton, J. Gordon. *The Encyclopedia of American Religions.* Wilmington, N.C.: McGrath Publishing Company, 1978.

Morrison, James H., and James Moreira, ed. *Tempered by Rum: Rum in the History of the Maritime Provinces.* Porters Lake, N.S.: Pottersfield Press, 1988.

Morton, W. L. *The Kingdom of Canada: A General History from the Earliest Time.* Toronto: McClelland and Stewart Limited, 1982.

Neft, David S. and Richard M. Cohen. *The Sports Encyclopedia: Baseball.* New York: St. Martin's Press, 1987.

Obojski, Robert. *Bush League: A History of Minor League Baseball.* New York: Macmillan Publishing Co., Inc., 1975.

O'Brien, T. C., ed. *The Encyclopedic Dictionary of the Western Churches.* Washington: Corpus Publications, 1970.

Offen, Neil. *God Save the Players: The Funny, Crazy, Sometimes Violent World of Sports Fans.* Chicago: Playboy Press, 1974.

Peterson, Robert. *Only the Ball Was White: A History of Legendary Black Players and All-black Professional Teams.* New York: McGraw-Hill, 1984.

Porteous, John. "We Was Here First." *Reader's Digest* (February 1974).

Quick, John. *Dictionary of Weapons and Military Terms.* New York: McGraw-Hill Inc., 1973.

Ruth, Claire. *The Babe and I.* Englewood, N. J.: Prentice Hall, Inc., 1959.

Schaap, Dick, ed. *Nobody Asked Me, But...The World of Jimmy Cannon.* New York: Penguin Books, 1978.

Seymour, Harold. *Baseball, The Early Years.* New York: Oxford University Press, 1960.

Shannon, Bill, and George Kalinsky. *The Ballparks.* New York: Hawthorn Books Inc., 1975.

Sharpe, Errol. *A People's History of Prince Edward Island.* Toronto: Steel Rail Publishing, 1976.

Shecter, Leonard. *The Jocks.* New York: Paperback Library, 1970.

Simpson, Kieran, ed. *Canadian Who's Who.* Toronto: University of Toronto Press, 1979.

Smith, Robert. *Babe Ruth's America.* New York: Crowell Publishers, 1974.

Tallman, R. D., and J. I. Tallman. "The Diplomatic Search for the St. Croix River. 1796-1798." *Acadiensis: Journal of the History of the Atlantic Region* (Spring 1972).

Thompson, Colleen. *New Brunswick Inside Out.* Ottawa: Waxwing Productions, 1977.

Thorn, John. *A Century of Baseball Lore.* New York: Hart Publishing Company, Inc. 1974.

————, and Pete Palmer. *Total Baseball.* New York: Warner Books, 1989.

Time-Life Books, ed. *1920-1930.* New York: Time-Life Books, 1969.

Unstead, R. J. *The Thirties.* Toronto: Macdonald Educational, 1974.

Veeck, Bill. *Veeck—As In Wreck.* New York: Ballintine Books, 1978.

Voigt, David Quentin. *American Baseball, From Gentleman's Sport to the Commissioner System.* University of Oklahoma Press, 1966.

Young, Peter, ed. *The World Almanac Book of World War II.* Englewood, N.J.: Prenctice-Hall Inc., 1981.

Interviews

Jim Mont was interviewed July 29, 1988, in his small downtown room in Halifax, N.S.

Ace Foley was interviewed July 30, 1988, in the newsroom of the *The Chronicle-Herald* and *The Mail-Star* in Halifax, N.S.

Lightning Amirault was interviewed August 1 and 2, 1988, in the television room of the Tital View Manor in Yarmouth, N.S.

Doug Horton was interviewed August 1, 1988 in the living room of his house in Yarmouth, N.S.

Haley Horton was interviewed August 1, 1988, in the kitchen of his house just outside Yarmouth, N.S.

Nate Bain was interviewed August 3, 1988, in his cabin at the Berwick Church Camp in Berwick, N.S.

Armond Wigglesworth was interviewed August 3, 1988, in the living room of his house in Summerville Beach, N.S.

Garneau Seaman was interviewed August 4, 1988, in his apartment in a senior citizens' complex in Liverpool, N.S.

Laurie Thorburne was interviewed August 4, 1988, in the living room of his house in Liverpool, N.S.

Colin Howell was interviewed July 31, 1988, on the backyard deck of his house in Darmouth, N.S.

Ackie Albon was interviewed August 5, 1988, in the living room of his house in Springhill, N.S.

Lawson Fowler was interviewed August 5, 1988, in the living room of his house in Springhill, N.S.

Leo MacDonald was interviewed August 5, 1988, in the living room of his house in Springhill, N.S.

Jim Morell was interviewed August 6, 1988, in the backyard of his house in Fredericton, N.B.

Lefty Brownell was interviewed August 6, 1988, in the kitchen of his house in Saint John, N.B.

Orville Mitchell was interviewed August 7 and 8, 1988, in the dining room of his house in St. Stephen, N.B.

Phil McCarroll was interviewed August 8, 1988, in the living room of his house in St. Stephen, N.B.

Gordon Coffey was interviewed August 8, 1988, in the living room of his house in St. Stephen, N.B.

George Purcell was interviewed August 9, 1988, on the porch of his house in St. Stephen, N.B.

Harry Boles was interviewed August 9, 1988, on the porch of his house in St. Stephen, N.B.

Squirrelly Ross was interviewed August 9, 1988, in the kitchen of his house in St. Stephen, N.B.

Lloyd Kelly was interviewed August 12, 1988, at the Royal Canadian Legion Hall in St. Stephen, N.B.

Ken Kallenburg was interviewed August 12, 1988, in the living room of his house in Calais, Me.

Roy Boles was interviewed August 12, 1989, in the kitchen of his house in Fort Erie, Ont.

Dick Granville was interviewed by telephone December 12, 1989, from his house in St. Stephen, N.B.

Phil Rouse was interviewed by telephone December 12, 1989, from his house in St. Stephen, N.B.

INDEX